Kellogg
on
Strategy

Kellogg on Strategy

Concepts, Tools, and Frameworks for Practitioners

DAVID DRANOVE

AND

SONIA MARCIANO

WILEY

John Wiley & Sons, Inc.

Published by John Wiley & Sons, Inc., Hoboken, New Jersey.
Published simultaneously in Canada.

For general information on our other products and services or for technical support, please contact our Customer Care Department within the United States at (800) 762-2974, outside the United States at (317) 572-3993 or fax (317) 572-4002.

Designations used by companies to distinguish their products are often claimed by trademarks. In all instances where the author or publisher is aware of a claim, the product names appear in Initial Capital letters. Readers, however, should contact the appropriate companies for more complete information regarding trademarks and registration.

Wiley also publishes its books in a variety of electronic formats. Some content that appears in print may not be available in electronic books. For more information about Wiley products, visit our web site at www.wiley.com.

Library of Congress Cataloging-in-Publication Data:

Dranove, David.
   Kellogg on strategy : concepts, tools, and frameworks for practitioners /
David Dranove and Sonia Marciano.
     p. cm.
   ISBN-13 978-0-471-47855-3 (cloth)
   ISBN-10 0-471-47855-5 (cloth)
   1. Strategic planning. 2. Strategic planning—Case studies. 3.
Industrial management. I. Marciano, Sonia. II. Title.
HD30.28.D72 2005
658.4'012—dc22

2005006853

Printed in the United States of America.

10 9 8 7 6 5 4 3 2 1

CONTENTS

1737

113120

Introduction

A Strategy Book for Strategists

We hear often from former students whose current jobs involve strategy formulation and evaluation. They are kind enough to tell us that the material taught in the Kellogg strategy curriculum has been incredibly relevant. But they also ask us many follow-up questions. They have mastered the basic academic concepts taught in a textbook strategy class, but they are worried about implementation. The questions we receive typically include:

- How can I be sure that my list of possible opportunities for value creation is accurate and complete?
- What structured approach should I use for choosing among these options?
- How do I know that I have done a thorough job of competitor analysis, and how do I select from the many recommended options for coping with market forces?
- How do I communicate my analysis to those who lead and to those expected to follow?

We have received enough inquiries like these to recognize the need for a strategy book for individuals who are informed about strategy—those who have MBAs, have read books on the topic, or are practitioners. This book is for these informed readers, who understand the high concepts of strategy but want to know better how to put these concepts into action.

In this book you will revisit the principles that guide strategy formulation. More importantly, you will find the tools and templates necessary for identifying and choosing among strategic alternatives. In effect, this is the strategy book you should read, now that you have identified what you want to know. This book lays out the steps required for formulating and analyzing strategy and tells you what the product of each step should look like. Following the processes outlined in this book will inform you of what you should do and why, and as a result your communication with others will be greatly enhanced.

FITTING INTO YOUR STRATEGY LIBRARY

The introductions of strategy books often suggest that the book you are holding is the only book on the topic you will ever need. Given that we are academics, it would be disingenuous for us to suggest you should own only one book on any topic of importance. However, we would like you to know how this book would fit into your *strategy library*. While there are a number of well-regarded strategy books, we have chosen a few that we believe are representative of books with particular points of view.

The popular *Execution: The Discipline of Getting Things Done* by Bossidy, Charan, and Burck,[1] reminds the reader of the chasm between a plan and the execution of that plan. Books such as this one enable the reader to benefit from decades of actual management experience. In this case, the authors relate many stories of strategies that succeeded or failed because of implementation, rather than the content of the strategy itself. This book provides a more vivid reality check than do academic books on strategy. However, the fact that good strategy will fail in the face of bad execution is evidence that strategy and execution are complementary, not that execution is more important than strategy development. (And we make no claim that strategy development is more important than execution.)

The importance of combining strategy formulation with execution is self-evident from many examples. Consider Dell and Gateway. Both firms pursued the same cost leadership strategy with different success. The strategic idea was simple and correct: Rapidly declining components costs meant that lean inventories would give mail order computer makers a decided cost advantage over manufacturers like Hewlett-Packard (HP), who sold their computers through bricks and mortar retailers. But Michael Dell understood that customers would be nervous about mail order quality, and executed his strategy by partnering with brand name component makers ("Intel inside") and setting up a top-notch rapid response call center. His early mover advantage—the result of a sound strategy and solid execution—allowed Dell to enjoy economies of scale in staffing the call center, further enhancing the cost advantage.

Not surprisingly, many famous books focus on strategy formulation. Quite a few suggest that success can be had by emulating the strategies of other successful firms. Examples include *Good to Great* by Collins, *The New Market Leaders* by Wiersema, and the seminal *In Search of Excellence* by Peters and Waterman.[2] We think that learning about winners (and losers, for that matter) can be highly informative, and much of what is taught in the Kellogg strategy curriculum is derived from case studies of particular firms. However, the danger of learning by observation is that one might not be careful to observe enough.

To see why simply emulating winners may be ineffective, consider the variety of strategies pursued by four highly regarded and successful firms: Trek, Usiminas, Wal-Mart, and Nordstrom.[3] Trek's success is built largely on low-cost outsourcing and careful brand management. Usiminas is a traditional vertically integrated steel firm best known for its operational excellence in manufacturing. That excellence, coupled with its access to Brazil's low-cost labor and abundant energy supplies, has made Usiminas one of the lowest-cost producers of steel in the world. Unlike the first two, Wal-Mart is a distributor and retailer. It relies on the initiative of its local store managers, combined with sophisticated purchasing and inventory management, to keep its retailing costs below those of its rivals. Nordstrom is another successful retailer, but it relies on innovative compensation to motivate a sales force that is second to none in the industry.

Given this variety, adopting a monkey see, monkey do approach to strategy would be frustrating. Should manufacturers outsource or integrate? Should retailers concentrate on distribution or sales? Compounding this frustration is the fact that we see poorly performing firms employing the same strategies as industry exemplars. For every Trek, there is a Raleigh; for every Usiminas, a Bethlehem Steel; for every Wal-Mart, a JCPenney; for every Nordstrom, a Carson Pirie Scott. The failures did not merely have poor execution. They often lacked the resources and capabilities necessary to make their strategies succeed. Careful examination of successful firms points out further dangers of emulating them. In the past few years, business publications have heaped praise on AOL, Hummer, Krispy Kreme, and others, only to wonder later, "What went wrong?" The sad fact is that a successful strategy at a given time or place may be the wrong strategy just a few years later or in a different environment. Strategy development is a continuous process that must be sensitive to idiosyncratic market conditions.

We do believe that it is useful to study the behaviors of firms. The value of this study is not in trying to develop lists of characteristics that lead to automatic success. *There is no such list.* Firms succeed because the strategies their managers choose best allow them to exploit the potential profit opportunities that exist at that time and as a result of their particular circumstances. We believe that we can better understand why firms succeed or fail when we analyze the decisions of specific firms at given points in time in terms of consistent principles of market economics and strategic action.

The best known strategy book that lays out a set of principles for strategy formulation is Porter's *Competitive Strategy*.[4] Like Porter, we take an economic approach to strategy—all of the principles that we present are supported by careful theoretical development and empirical research that has been subject to withering peer review prior to publication. The textbook we use at Kellogg, *The Economics of Strategy* by Besanko, Dranove, Shanley, and Schaefer,[5] expands on Porter's concepts, including positioning analysis and industry analysis. But strategy practitioners need more than concepts. As our former students remind us, the practitioner needs to know *how* to develop a sensible strategy, and not just why a strategy makes sense.

This book fills that void. In each chapter, we present strategy concepts grounded in economic theory. We also show how to take these concepts and use them to evaluate all of the key elements of strategy. Thus, we describe in detail the *why* and *how* of:

• Evaluating your firm's strategic position.
• Performing industry analysis.

- Assessing competitive pressure and evaluating responses to competitor price and nonprice strategies.
- Coping with entry.
- Establishing a long-term sustainable competitive advantage.

Each chapter contains actionable advice not only for making decisions with greater clarity, but also for communicating the logic of the firm's choices to people inside and outside of the organization. This is the book that our former Kellogg students have asked for. And we have learned to trust their judgment.

NOTES

1. L. Bossidy, R. Charan, and C. Burck, *Execution: The Discipline of Getting Things Done*, New York: Crown Business, 2002.

2. J. C. Collins. *Good to Great*, New York: Harper Business, 2001. F. Wiersema, *The New Market Leaders,* New York: Free Press, 2001. T. J. Peters and R. H. Waterman, *In Search of Excellence*, New York: Harper and Row, 1982.

3. The full name of Usiminas is Usinas Siderurgicas de Minas Gerais.

4. M. Porter, *Competitive Strategy*, New York: Free Press, 1980.

5. D. Besanko, D. Dranove, M. Shanley, and S. Schaefer, *Economics of Strategy*, New York: Wiley, 2003.

CHAPTER 1

GETTING READY TO
DO STRATEGY

$\mathbf{I}$n the early 1990s, the Allegheny
Hospital Education and Research Foundation (AHERF) launched a
strategy to become a large integrated health care delivery system.
AHERF was not the only health care provider pursuing this strategy. In
fact, this was the dominant strategic direction proposed by industry analysts and managers alike. Within a few years, AHERF was one of the
largest integrated health care providers in the United States and its
CEO was hailed as a visionary. By 1998, AHERF was also bankrupt.

In the early 2000s, Samsung Corporation launched a strategy to revi-
talize its consumer video electronics business. Long regarded as a low-
quality brand, it sought a quality leadership position in the fledgling
market for digital home entertainment, including high definition television (HDTV). Samsung embraced digital light processing (DLP) technology.[1] Cheaper and fatter than plasma, more expensive and thinner than
traditional rear projection televisions (RPTVs), Samsung's DLP televisions offered a picture quality that equaled or beat either alternative.[2]

Samsung's first generation DLP sets garnered rave reviews from specialty magazines and web sites. The technology appealed to critical early
HDTV adopters who did their research and ignored the brand reputation. In fact, Samsung's reputation has improved since the launch of
DLP. It has successfully entered the market for high-end DVD players
and is poised to compete in the high-end plasma market.

It takes little imagination to come up with a strategy. In fact, almost
all managers can easily identify any number of strategic options for their

firms. Here are a few popular business strategies, with examples of firms that have pursued them:

- Grow larger (General Electric, AHERF).
- Downsize (Avon, Sara Lee).
- Diversify into new markets (Wal-Mart, PepsiCo).
- Dominate a niche (Starbucks, Jiffy Lube).
- Outsource the production process (Nike, IKEA).
- Integrate the production process (Armani, Tiffany).
- Become the cost leader, even if quality is sacrificed (Kia, Motel 6).
- Become the quality leader, even if costs increase (BMW, Four Seasons Hotels, Samsung).
- Drive rivals from the market (Philip Morris, Microsoft).
- Cooperate with rivals (Philip Morris, Sony).
- Be an innovator (Intel, Philips Electronics).
- Be an imitator (Microsoft, Dell Computer).

While it may be easy to come up with a strategy, it is much more difficult to select the appropriate one. For every Samsung, there is an AHERF. Some consultants may offer compelling arguments in favor of one strategy; others may recommend the diametrically opposite strategy. To make things more confusing, what works for one firm may not work for another firm in the *same* industry. So while it may take little imagination to come up with a strategy, it may take a lot of hard work to come up with the optimal strategy.

In brief, you are describing a strategy when you do both of the following:

1. Describe in what respect your firm's output is truly unique (what is the product market in which your firm has a monopoly, if you will) or the process by which you achieve *inimitable* efficiency.
2. Describe how you plan to defend this unique product or process from competition, entry, and imitation.

This book presents analyses that help you clearly identify your current or intended "monopoly" position.

DOING STRATEGY

This book is about the process of developing and analyzing strategies. It presents the principles, tools, and templates necessary for choosing among strategic alternatives. The goal of this process (often called strategic analysis or strategy evaluation) is to answer the following two principal questions (the PQs):

1. *Does the firm possess advantages that will translate into profits?*

   To answer this question, we need to identify what the firm brings to the market that enables it to outperform its rivals. The firm may have a superior quality product that the market deems worthy of a price premium. Or the firm may have a superior production process that gives it a cost advantage.

2. *Does the firm's business environment permit these advantages to turn into profits?*

   High quality and low costs are no guarantee of profits. It is essential to identify characteristics of the firm's environment that enable it to prosper from its advantages. Through an understanding of the business environment, we can answer questions such as how competition might erode profits, what firms can do about rivalry, and how the firm can sustain its profits over the long haul.

There are several reasons why the PQs are the right questions to ask when analyzing strategic alternatives:

1. Answering the PQs gives managers a more thorough understanding of the process by which their firm creates wealth and the conditions upon which that process depends.
2. This deep understanding is necessary to insure that managers do not change strategic direction for the sake of change, rather than in response to genuine problems and challenges.
3. By answering the PQs, managers can better determine whether a chosen strategy directly addresses the problems at hand. Willy-nilly selection of a strategy, whether because it sounds good or because it has become the latest fad, is not likely to bear fruit.

Evaluating and making strategic choices on the basis of how they resolve the PQs will lead to enduring profits.

4. The very process of answering the PQs often generates strategic choices. Strategy may thus be thought of as an organic process, in which choices emerge during the analytic process. We will encounter numerous examples in which the correct strategic responses are revealed through the analysis of the PQs.

5. Correct analysis leads to effective tactical choices, effective because managers are more likely to choose actions that enhance and leverage the firm's true advantage while properly accounting for competitive responses.

A HOMEWORK ASSIGNMENT

Since this book is, in effect, a course in strategy, we think it is helpful to pull from our Kellogg course syllabus, specifically the section describing the homework assignments:

> The evaluation of a firm's strategy will not be satisfied by phrases such as "superior marketing," "superior inventory management," or "superior product variety." The answer to the two key strategy evaluation questions needs to be 7 to 10 single-spaced typewritten pages.

Not to worry; you won't owe us assignments. However, contrast the richness of a 7- to 10-page single-spaced strategic analysis to the platitudes that often follow when managers are asked, "What are this firm's advantages?" or "How competitive is the market?"

This chapter lays out a broad game plan for answering the PQs. The rest of the book fills in the details and offers numerous examples of strategy in action. Chapters 2 to 4 address primarily the first of the two questions; Chapters 5 to 8 turn to the second question. Chapter 9 concludes with two highly detailed strategy evaluations, one for Amazon.com and one for the Chicago hospital market. While these analyses are fairly thorough, we were limited to public information. A manager performing the analysis on his or her own firm could probe more deeply.

We offer a caveat before we proceed. We acknowledge that a one-size-fits-all framework for strategy evaluation is too much to promise. On the other hand, teaching strategy evaluation exclusively by example may leave the reader inspired but apprehensive about how to initiate his or her own analysis. Hence, we propose a set of *general* tools and frameworks, but remind the reader that they may need to be adapted to his or her own *particular* strategic situations.

One more caveat: The methods that we present can appear daunting in their richness. We offer detailed guidance on how to perform much of the analysis forthcoming, but not all of it. It would be impractical to incorporate all the tools needed to do strategy evaluation in one book. Furthermore, any text suggesting it has enough information to guide one through the entire process is likely to be overreaching. Many good sources exist for topics not fully developed in this book and where appropriate, we point you to them.

STEP ONE: ORGANIZE THE INFORMATION REQUIRED FOR STRATEGY ANALYSIS

Strategy should be driven by facts: facts about the firm, facts about its rivals, and facts about consumers. No amount of economic theory or consulting templates can substitute for institutional knowledge. But "institutional knowledge" is a broad concept, seemingly without bounds. Moreover, that knowledge is often disorganized and scattered. With a little discipline, it is possible to organize this knowledge to greatly facilitate the process of developing strategy.

In thinking about organizing knowledge, remember that the goal of strategic analysis is to help a particular firm determine how best to generate revenues that exceed its costs, including its capital costs. In our experience, managers often begin their analysis with *qualitative claims* about their firm that cannot be substantiated by *quantitative data* about the firm's actual performance. Hence, a good way to start organizing knowledge is by examining actual financial performance, preferably as close to the business unit level as possible.

We believe that the best measures identify what is commonly known as *economic profit*.[3] Figure 1.1 presents one version of how to measure economic profit, as well as a list of its common sources of economic

Figure 1.1
Economic Profit and Its Sources[a]

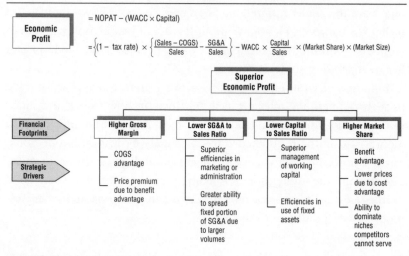

$$= \text{NOPAT} - (\text{WACC} \times \text{Capital})$$

$$= \left\{ (1 - \text{tax rate}) \times \left\{ \frac{(\text{Sales} - \text{COGS})}{\text{Sales}} - \frac{\text{SG\&A}}{\text{Sales}} \right\} - \text{WACC} \times \frac{\text{Capital}}{\text{Sales}} \right\} \times (\text{Market Share}) \times (\text{Market Size})$$

COGS: Cost of goods sold.
SG&A: Selling, general, and administrative expenses.
WACC: Weighted average cost of capital (an interest rate that is commensurate with the amount of risk taken on in this product market).
Capital: The book value of the assets the firm needs to participate in this product market.

[a]We are grateful to David Besanko for his permission to use this schematic.

profit. Professor David Besanko, one of the creators of the core strategy course at Kellogg, developed this schematic to introduce students to the topic of strategy. The top equation states that economic profit equals net operating profits after tax (NOPAT) minus a charge for the capital tied up in the weighted average cost of capital (WACC). The equation just below it divides these terms into their components, each of which can be thought of as a metric or financial footprint of superior economic profit.

The schematic shows that a firm cannot generate superior economic profits unless it can map its advantage into some metric or footprint (such as gross margin or SG&A/Sales) in which it outperforms the average of a firm in the same business. By knowing which driver(s) is the basis for the firm's superior performance, the firm is guided in protecting and leveraging its advantage. Begin your strategy process by computing your economic profit and then list the strategic drivers that contribute toward your success.

Calculating economic profits and identifying the footprints of economic advantage, by business unit if possible, is certainly not a trivial task. However, this is also essential to any meaningful strategy. We would be highly skeptical if a firm laid claim to a strategic advantage over its rivals but could not back up the claim with financial metrics or economic analysis. Strategy formulation that started with such a questionable premise of superiority would not hold water. Not all firms have the financial and accounting systems that permit convincing analyses along these lines, but the more that a firm relies on using financial measurement as a compass for strategic choices, the better it will become. Starting with poor information and developing the necessary systems over time surely beats ignoring the analysis altogether.

The second exercise useful for organizing information is called a "firm map." A useful map depicts the firm's position in its industry, as shown in Figure 1.2. Each stage in the map represents an industry or a set of firms whose outputs are considered reasonably close substitutes by customers. In the vertical chain (from Stage 1 to Stage 4), the industries are ordered from least to most processed (i.e., from furthest to closest to the end customers), and the dots represent particular firms in the industry. Firms in each stage supply the firms in the next, while firms in the final stage sell to consumers. While the firms in any one stage may have multiple suppliers, this analysis should focus on the most critical suppliers. We have arbitrarily determined that our firm of interest is in Stage 3. We have circled one of the dots in Stage 3 to indicate the location of our firm. The firm map shows that our firm (and all others in Stage 3) obtains supplies from three industries (A, B, and C).

Along the vertical and horizontal axis of each box are the characteristics that consumers value most highly and use to distinguish among firms. In this example, we have chosen perceived value on the X-axis and product variety on the Y-axis of the box for Stage 3. We see that our firm is fairly high in value but low in variety. We could have incorporated a third dimension by varying the size of the dots used to identify each firm. The size of the dots might correlate to market share or annual sales. Quite frankly, the analyst can get as creative and colorful as the availability of data allows.

The remaining boxes depict industries whose outputs substitute for

Figure 1.2
The Firm Map

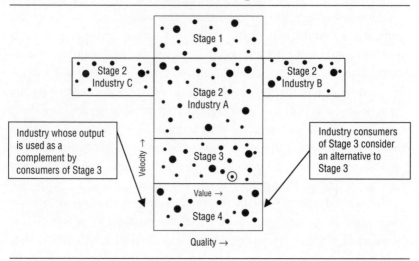

or are complementary to the output of our industry.[4] When complete, the boxes capture all competitors, substitutes, and complements. For example, Hyatt Hotels and Sheraton Hotels are in the same industry box (hotels), campgrounds are a substitute, and the availability of rental cars is a complement.

Like our financial analysis, firm mapping requires a measure of diligence. It is possible to prepare a qualitative firm map based on institutional knowledge. We offer a number of tools for adding rigor to the mapping exercise: Chapter 4 shows how to quantify a firm's position in the market, and Chapter 5 discusses how to more precisely identify competitors. The marketing literature also offers guidance on a number of mapping issues.[5]

Understanding the facts about your firm's position is an indispensable part of strategic formulation, and you should attempt to make a map even if you know it is imperfect. Like the analysis of economic profits, something is better than nothing. *Do not neglect your obligation to organize essential institutional knowledge as a central component of strategy formulation and analysis. The lack of perfect information is no excuse.*

STEP TWO: DEFINE THE FIRM'S POSITION

To enjoy superior economic profits, a firm must have either a superior position in an industry that generates average returns (e.g., Wal-Mart), or an average position in an industry that generates superior returns (e.g., Eli Lilly). Having a superior position in a superior industry (Microsoft) is rare and especially profitable. The next two steps in the strategy process involve examining the firm's position relative to its industry, and examining the overall industry profitability. We present positioning before industry analysis, but this choice is arbitrary.

The first step in positioning analysis is identifying the firm's customers. The firm mapping should provide this information. The next step is to determine the firm's *value creation proposition*, that is, how the firm creates benefits for consumers (B) above and beyond the cost of production (C). At a minimum, the firm needs to generate a positive B–C. If it cannot do so, it may as well shut down.

Chapter 2 develops the B–C framework thoroughly. In Chapter 2, we argue that it is not sufficient for a firm to produce a positive B–C. If the firm is to outperform its rivals, it must produce more B–C than they do. The chapter then uses B–C to explain a number of concepts that are fundamental to strategy, including generic strategies and disruptive technologies. Increasing B–C is not just a matter of what the firm does, but also about whom the firm chooses to serve. Finding the right customer means segmenting the marketing correctly.[6] After discussing segmentation, the chapter closes by offering a variety of tactics for creating B–C and discussing how firms should set their prices to best exploit their B–C advantage.

Under the right circumstances, firms can convert B–C into profits for their owners or shareholders. Chapter 3 identifies these circumstances through the lens of a powerful theory known as the "resource-based view of the firm." The resource-based view holds that the translation from B–C to profits depends on whether the firm's value creation process is proprietary. For a firm to profit from B–C, it must possess resources and capabilities that are scarce, immobile, and scopable. Chapter 3 clarifies these concepts and offers a "resources and capabilities audit" that the analyst should use to fully gauge a firm's strengths. A detailed example of Disney's animated motion picture division illustrates how to use the audit. As we have already mentioned, there is no substitute for institutional knowledge, and it cannot be emphasized enough that the results of this type of analysis must be consistent with the facts. Otherwise, a firm can delude itself into overestimating its strengths and fail to take appropriate actions.

This analysis is often largely qualitative, consisting of lists of resources and capabilities and subjective assessments of the resulting value creation proposition. Chapter 4 presents tools from economics, accounting, and marketing research that the analyst may use to quantify value creation. With this final step, the analyst can identify the firm's strategic position with some degree of certainty. Such an analysis will be a vast improvement over the type of cursory positioning statement that often underlies strategic thinking.

STEP THREE: INDUSTRY ANALYSIS

Each firm belongs to a particular stage in its overall market. Industry analysis is a tool for assessing the profitability of that stage by considering the environment in which the firms in that stage compete. This analysis should provide a very clear sense of what is positive and negative about the environment. (All too often, industry analysis devolves into a litany of negatives; this is a temptation that must be avoided.) By far the most popular tool for industry analysis is Michael Porter's five forces framework.

The five forces framework begins with market definition, a tool that we develop in Chapter 5. Porter's framework then posits a simple hypothetical: Suppose that an industry creates positive B–C. Given this hypothetical, the framework identifies five environmental forces that could cause this industry to earn zero economic profits, despite creating positive value. The five forces are:

1. *Internal Rivalry:* Competition among firms in the industry can drive prices down toward costs. Consumers end up enjoying all the value created by the industry.

2. *Entry:* Industry profits act as a siren call to new firms. Their entry erodes the profits of incumbents by stealing market share and intensifying price competition.

3. *Substitutes:* These also steal market share, and the distinction between substitutes and competitors/entrants is often a matter of degree.

4. *Supplier Power:* This refers to the power of suppliers to command high prices for their inputs. A powerful supplier can extract all the profits from its trading partners, who may have no alternative but to accede to the demanded price or go out of business altogether.

5. *Buyer Power:* Buyer power is symmetric to supplier power. A powerful buyer can demand steep discounts and if its suppliers have nowhere else to turn, they will be forced to accept them.

Chapters 5 to 7 detail the factors that contribute to internal rivalry and entry, drawing heavily on economic theories of competition. We view internal rivalry as a kind of industry cancer. Chapter 5 offers a variety of ways to diagnose the disease and Chapter 6 offers suggested cures. In Chapter 7, we describe how to assess the threat of entry and steps that firms may take to prevent it. These chapters contain checklists that will assist in assessing how these forces may affect industry profits.

Here are some checklists for assessing the remaining forces. The distinction between substitutes and internal rivalry/entry is often a matter of degree and often requires little further elaboration. The analyst who wishes to give due consideration to the topic of substitutes should be sure to complete the checklist shown in Table 1.1.

Tables 1.2 and 1.3 offer checklists for the analysis of supplier and buyer power. A thorough analysis of supplier and buyer power requires a range of subtle analytic tools that are beyond the scope of this book. These topics are treated in great detail in *The Economics of Strategy*, however. (This is the textbook that we use in our core strategy class.) You may wish to refer to the textbook for the analytic details.

Consonance analysis is another framework that may be used to get a sense of the overarching features of an industry.[7] Like the five forces, consonance analysis begins with market definition. The analyst then describes how firms in the market create value for their consumers, that is,

Table 1.1
Factors Affecting Pressure from Substitutes

Factor	Comment
Are close substitutes available?	If yes, industry price is tempered by substitute's price.
Do substitutes offer high value for the price?	If yes, industry price is tempered.
Does the industry face a high price elasticity of demand?	If yes, this would indicate that consumers are willing to purchase substitute.

Table 1.2
Factors Affecting Power of Input Suppliers

Factor	Comment
Is supplier industry more concentrated than industry it sells to?	If yes, then competition among suppliers may be limited, and their power enhanced.
Do firms in industry purchase small volumes relative to other customers of the supply industry?	If yes, then industry may have to pay premium prices and obtain inferior trade terms relative to other customers.
Are there few substitutes for the supplier's input?	If yes, then supplier can hold out for higher price.
Do firms in industry make investments that are specific to their relationship with suppliers?	If yes, then industry may be tied to its suppliers and unable to turn elsewhere if supply prices increase.
Do suppliers pose a credible threat of forward integration into the industry?	If yes, then industry may have to accede to price increases or invite forward integration.
Are suppliers able to price discriminate on the basis of ability/willingness to pay?	If yes, suppliers can extract profits from the firms that most highly value the inputs.

Table 1.3
Factors Affecting Power of Buyers

Factor	Comment
Is buyer industry more concentrated than industry it sells to?	If yes, then competition among buyers may be limited, and their power enhanced.
Do buyers purchase in large volumes?	If yes, then buyers may be able to negotiate favorable prices and trade terms.
Can buyers find substitutes?	If yes, then industry pricing is tempered by availability of substitutes.
Do firms in industry make investments that are specific to their relationship with buyers?	If yes, then industry may be tied to its buyers and unable to turn elsewhere if prices decrease.
Do buyers pose a credible threat of backward integration into the industry?	If yes, then industry may have to accede to price decreases or invite backward integration.
Are suppliers able to price discriminate on the basis of ability/willingness to pay?	If yes, suppliers can extract profits from the firms that most highly value the inputs.
Does the industry's product represent a significant fraction of the buyer's cost?	If yes, buyer will be aggressive in seeking discounts.
Are buyers able to negotiate prices on a transaction by transaction basis?	If yes, buyers may be able to extract price concessions from the most vulnerable sellers.

how they create B. Similarly, the analyst describes the factors that affect costs. Next, the analyst identifies emerging trends that will affect the creation of B and C.

"Consonance" means agreement or harmony. The goal of consonance analysis is to determine whether the activities that firms in the industry use to create B and C are aligned with the conditions in which the industry operates. If value creating activities are consonant with industry conditions, then the industry has greater potential to create value (create B–C). Likewise, if a firm's value creating activities are consonant with industry conditions, that firm is well-positioned to create value. In this way, consonance analysis is more oriented toward firm-level analysis than is the five forces framework, because the latter considers the conditions facing a typical firm, not necessarily one particular firm.

Consider the pharmaceutical industry, which until the 1980s created B largely by a system of "informed trial and error" that screened hundreds of thousands of compounds for their medical effects and moved a few dozen of the most promising through a lengthy and costly process of clinical trials. For some time, this was not consonant with ongoing changes in clinical science that enabled researchers to better predict the effects of compounds on the basis of theoretical models. The result was the emergence of small companies that specialized in early stage research. Many of today's most successful drugs were first discovered by these small companies, and much of the industry's wealth has migrated in that direction as well. Even so, many pharmaceutical companies developed new value creation tools in response to the change in scientific regimes. A good example is Merck, which borrowed tools from financial economics to align its drug development budgeting methods with the new realities of how scientific knowledge was emerging.[8] These methods became the paradigm for the industry.

A final framework we mention here (although there are several more) is SWOT analysis. SWOT stands for "Strengths, Weaknesses, Opportunities, and Threats." This framework is very commonly used by companies at off-site strategy retreats. At the breakout sessions, participants are given four flip charts, one for *S*, and so on, and asked to identify the firm's SWOT. Everyone brainstorms for five minutes and then makes their list. Like any other framework for industry analysis, rigor and deep analysis have a payoff. If ideas are off the cuff and unsubstantial, the output of the analysis will not be valuable. Fortunately, there are sound theoretical underpinnings to SWOT analysis. You might consider the *SW* to be akin to positioning analysis and the *OT* to be much like the industry analysis. The tools and frameworks we present in this book should help any manager produce a stellar SWOT analysis.

STEP FOUR: EVALUATE SUSTAINABILITY

It is one thing for a firm to outperform its rivals in the short run. It is quite another to secure an advantage that lasts for many years. Entry is one of the major threats to sustaining an advantage. Chapter 8 describes many other challenges to sustaining advantage. Some of the factors that we discuss in Chapter 8 are:

- Is there a learning curve that confers an advantage on the firms with the most experience?
- Are there switching costs that make it difficult for newcomers to steal the customers of incumbent firms?
- Does reputation affect demand and supply relationships?
- Does the market display "network effects," whereby consumers lock onto a single product design or technology standard?

Some of these factors are associated with the topic of "early mover advantages"—those advantages enabling firms to continue to outperform the competition well after achieving early success. But firms need not be first to the market to enjoy sustained advantages. Look no further than Microsoft, Wal-Mart, and Southwest Airlines for famous examples of successful second (or later) movers.

No assessment of a firm's strategy is complete without careful attention to sustainability. Chapters 7 and 8 discuss how firms can create sustainable advantages. But advantaged firms are vulnerable due to the myriad factors that tend to reduce excess returns over time. The five forces must be kept at bay, and the factors that permit a sustained advantage (e.g., reputation effects) can deteriorate over time. There can be shocks, or changes, in the general environment. While all firms in an industry are affected by shocks, they are not all affected the same. Firm level choices with respect to particular trading partners, location, product/service features, and so on affect how one firm is affected relative to the industry as a whole. At the same time, deterioration (or improvement) can be the result of purely firm level factors. Chapter 8 discusses many of these effects.

WRAP-UP: THE STRATEGY TOP 10

Several times during the course we like to remind students of the main course concepts—the Strategy Top 10.[9] See how these 10 concepts resonate with your understanding of your own firm's strategy:

1. Firms exist to turn shareholders' resources into profits. While other imperatives frequently emerge, the best leaders resist getting sidetracked. If the initiative is not about creating shareholder wealth, it is ill-advised. This is absolutely not the same as saying the firm's environmental impact or reputation vis à vis labor or other such concerns are unimportant. This is to say that any initiative must be understood in the context of converting shareholder resources into profits over the long run.

2. The firm must have a *unique and defensible value creation proposition.* One can conceive of ways to create value but not profits. If a network creates a hit TV show only to lose all of its profits to the show's stars and writers, that network might have done well to consider how it was going to retain, as profits, the value it created.
   - Does the firm create value from the perspective of some consumers?
   - Can the firm's activities be imitated?
   - If the firm does not own the productive resource, can the owner expropriate the value away from the firm?

3. If the firm's uniquely valuable role is that it is better at something, it should leverage this advantage in as many markets as possible. Be sure to identify all the markets in which you can leverage your advantage. Some firms appear to be operating in disparate businesses and thereby defying the hackneyed strategist's advice to stay focused. However, disparate businesses may, in fact, rely on similar competencies or assets. The best opportunities are not necessarily in the same market, but do

leverage the source of the firm's current success. Using the analyses suggested here will help your firm identify what it might leverage.

4. Clarifying the preceding, the goal of strategy is to maximize economic profits through time, not to grow! Firms should grow into new markets or new activities only if there are synergies with their existing activities. If the firm's unique role is that it is different, the firm should optimize its activities to that difference and be careful not to overgrow. Consider the effect of growing in a particular way on the equation given previously for economic profits. Are the sales being added actually reducing profits? This is more than entirely possible!

5. Firms should be diligent to understand and, whenever possible, document the sources of their advantage. Nearly all managers claim that their firms are positioned to outperform their rivals. This is a statistical impossibility. Does the analysis suggested enable you to articulate your monopoly? Is the market you monopolize as valuable as you want to believe?

6. From a firm's point of view, the key question of *industry analysis* is: Can the firm define a uniquely valuable role in its industry?

   • If yes, rivalry and entry threats are lowered, as the firm has a unique position relative to current and potential competitors.
   • If yes, buyer and supplier power are lowered, as the firm fills a unique role for them.
   • Consonance analysis considers whether this unique role is consistent with long-term trends in consumer tastes, technology, and so on.
   • A uniquely valuable role requires a firm to be different from or better than the competition.

7. This is clear from the central position of rivalry in the industry analysis framework already presented, and certainly merits repeating: Firms must avoid destructive price competition, which is always a lose-lose proposition. If each firm has a uniquely valuable position, price competition is minimized, and each firm profits by serving its role. If not, you must find ways to soften price competition.

8. As indicated previously, a positioning statement is a statement of relatives. A firm's position can be expressed only relative to other firms. In developing strategy, never take competitors' positions as given or fixed. While it can be tough to anticipate the actions and reactions of rivals, it is important to make intelligent conjectures by stepping into their shoes.

9. In situations of high risk, evaluate strategies more on the extent to which they create or destroy *options* and less on a single prediction of their expected value. That is, take the economic profit equation given earlier and project the effect of your initiative over time. Does taking a hit in the near term give you a good vantage point in the future?

10. There are situations in which building market share is strategically important for future profits. These are first-mover advantages: learning curves, reputation effects, switching costs, and network effects (the power of all of these is discussed throughout this book). Firms must recognize when these situations do and *do not exist*, to avoid choosing the wrong tactics.

Does your firm follow these guidelines? If so, then you are likely on the right strategic course. This book can reinforce what you already know about strategy and help you refine your strategic choices when appropriate. If not, do not despair. We provide the details necessary to work through the Strategy Top 10, offer frameworks for assessing strategic choices, and help put your firm on course for strategic success.

NOTES

1. Texas Instruments holds the patent on the DLP processing chip and supplies several other brands, including Panasonic, Mitsubishi, and Gateway.

2. A 61-inch Samsung DLP set retails for about $3,000, versus $10,000 for a typical 60-inch plasma and $2,000 for a typical 60-inch RPTV.

3. Many consulting firms have their own proprietary measures. The most well known is Stern Stewart's Economic Value Added (EVA). However, there are many alternative ways to measure firm performance that take into account the opportunity cost of the firm's capital. Essentially, the difference between accounting profits and economic

profits is that the latter subtracts these operating costs (the book value of the firm's assets multiplied by an appropriate weighted average cost of capital (WACC). There is a large literature on this subject. The web site for the consulting firm Marakon (www.marakon.com) offers some good background reading on this subject.

4. A substitute industry sells something consumers consider an alternative to our firm's output but not as close an alternative as what our rivals or competitors sell. Complements enhance demand for the output of our industry.

5. For example, Professor George Day of the Wharton School Department of Marketing has a chapter on this in the book *Wharton on Dynamic Competitive Strategy* (Wiley).

6. There are many sources outside this text to learn about market segmentation, including *Kellogg on Marketing*.

7. The term "consonance" is usually attributed to Rumelt; however, the consonance analysis we describe here is a compilation of a variety of frameworks including Rumelt's framework and a framework developed by Kellogg faculty members.

8. Merck adapted the economics of real options to the budgeting process. It understood that investing in drug development was analogous to investing in options. Merck could "call" the option (i.e., increase the investment) at any time. Optimal investments depended on how scientific knowledge evolved. Some investments were necessary in order to obtain valuable information, and as new evidence altered assessments of the drug's potential, development budgets were altered according to complex formulae.

9. Thanks to David Besanko for coining this expression and developing the list.

CHAPTER 2

B Minus C: Positioning Your Firm against the Competition

Core Competencies

Every manager knows the strategist's mantra:

"To be successful, your firm must have a core competency."

The concept of core competencies is pervasive. We conducted an online search of business publications in 2003 and found more than 3,000 articles containing the term. (Another 3,000 mention "competencies," apparently taking for granted that they were "core.") Many of these articles identify the core competencies that make specific firms successful. South African life insurance company Citadel's core competency is its advice. BlueCat Network's core competency is "developing high quality software." Indeed, most managers can readily identify the core competencies of their own firms.

The term "core competencies" has exploded onto the strategy scene in just a few years. When we searched for articles published in 1990, we found only 10 that mention the term. While the term is new, the underlying concept is not. Strategists have put new words to an old concept and that old concept is as simple as it gets: To be successful, firms have to do something well. If there is any nuance in the current incarnation of this concept, it is that firms should not do the things that they do badly.

Unfortunately, strategic thinking often fails to extend beyond making a list of things done well. Managers often make such lists during the dreaded SWOT analysis breakout session of a firm's annual retreat (see Chapter 1). Such an exercise has some value, if only to stimulate discussion. But analysis of core competencies cannot be boiled down to a few minutes of list making and an hour of discussion. It takes considerable time to come up with a defensible, quantifiable list of core competencies. Once the competencies have been identified, there are many additional issues to be reckoned with that are usually ignored.

The rest of this chapter provides an intellectual foundation for the concept of "doing things well" and introduces a framework for analyzing strategy that accommodates specific concepts such as core competencies, as well as many other popular strategic concepts. We call this the B–C ("B minus C") framework. Because the B–C framework is both powerful and general, we think it is an ideal tool for organizing strategic analysis. As a way of motivating the B–C framework, we begin by discussing the sometimes shaky relationship between core competencies and profits.

COMPETENCIES AND PROFITS

Core competencies do not guarantee profits, as many examples prove. Throughout the 1990s, American Airlines ranked among industry leaders in efficiency and customer satisfaction, and its Sabre subsidiary has the best computerized reservation system in the industry. Even so, prolonged industry pricing woes nearly forced American to join many of its competitors in seeking bankruptcy protection. For more than three decades, pharmaceutical giant Merck has led the industry in research and development expertise and output. But Merck has lost patent protection on most of its successful drugs and currently faces the same fate for cholesterol blocker Zocor, the world's second leading selling drug. Many wonder if its pipeline of new drugs is strong enough for Merck to maintain its elevated status. We could go on and on—competencies do not guarantee profits.

One reason for the frequent disconnect between core competencies and profits is that several firms may possess the same competencies, leading to destructive competition. American is not the only hub and spoke carrier. Merck is not the only pharmaceutical company researching cholesterol reduction. Even firms that seem to enjoy a dominant market position can see their dominance erode over time, as new firms enter the market. In video gaming, Atari begat Nintendo, which begat the Sony Playstation and the Xbox. In desktop computing, Xerox was the real innovator, but was followed by IBM, which then saw a stream of low priced imitators: Leading Edge, Compaq, Dell, and Gateway. Some incumbents seem to enjoy long spells of dominance—think Alcoa Aluminum or Starbucks coffee—but successful incumbents should always expect other firms to try to grab some of the profits for themselves.

Even in the absence of competition and entry, firms with core competencies often fail to prosper. Most major league baseball teams attract millions of fans every year and receive nonstop media coverage. Yet most teams lose money, while many of their employees (the players) reap small fortunes. There are many other examples of firms that are squeezed by their top employees (hospitals, law firms, and universities among them). The problem these firms face is that they have not tied up the key assets that create their competence.

Still other firms are squeezed by distributors or retailers. Just ask any firm that sells to Wal-Mart whether it is easy to turn a profit. Wal-Mart accounts for nearly 10 percent of all nonauto related retail sales in the United States, and Wal-Mart customers do not take much notice of who makes the products that Wal-Mart sells. It is sufficient for the brand to have some credibility, and for the price to be extremely low. This gives Wal-Mart the upper hand when negotiating with competing vendors, so much so that Wal-Mart's "take no prisoners" negotiation style with vendors is legendary. In fact, not only does Wal-Mart obtain deep discounts from its suppliers, it forces them to invest in distribution techniques that *hold down Wal-Mart's costs*. Just like baseball teams that do not control their key asset (the athletes), consumer goods suppliers do not control a key asset (the channels offered by Wal-Mart). The result is the same: Profits are hard to come by.

These examples show that for a firm to be profitable, it is not enough to possess a competency (i.e., do something well). The following must also be true:

- The firm must avoid the ravages of competition.
- The firm must survive the threat of entry.
- The firm must control the assets that determine the value of its competence.

These are not the only limitations of the competency concept. There are a host of issues associated with putting the concept of competencies into practice. How does a firm identify a competency? How does it acquire it? How does it know that the competency is genuine?

Fortunately, we can deepen our understanding by turning to a basic concept in microeconomics: the concept of value creation. In our view, this simple economic idea can serve as the foundation for all of strategy. In the remainder of this chapter, we lay out the key economic principles of value creation. In Chapter 3, we present the *resource-based view of the firm*, a powerful theory that clarifies how value is converted into profits.

VALUE CREATION: THE KEY TO PROFITABILITY

We begin our economic analysis by defining value:

> Value is the difference between the benefits enjoyed by a firm's customers and its cost of production.

There are other ways to define value, and we do not claim that ours is the only reasonable definition. However, this particular definition leads to many insights, and that is why we like it. Perhaps the most important of these insights is expressed by the following proposition relating positioning to value creation:

> A firm in a competitive market can earn a profit only if it creates more value than its rivals.

To understand why this is true, it is helpful to discuss a few preliminaries regarding the concepts of costs and benefits.

A firm's costs include all expenses associated with production, including the cost of capital.[1] A good cost accountant can help a firm compute its costs. Benefits can be thought of as the value (measured in monetary terms) that the customer derives from consuming the firm's output. When measuring benefits, it is important to deduct any offsetting inconveniences. Sometimes, benefits and inconveniences are easily measured in dollars. A good example is the fuel savings enjoyed by consumers who purchase Toyota's Prius hybrid car, or the hundreds of dollars in increased fuel costs for those who purchase a Hummer H2 sports utility vehicle.

More often than not, benefits and inconveniences are intangible. The Prius offers owners the piece of mind that comes with a car that receives top marks for reliability. But Prius owners must also accept modest performance and limited luxury appointments. The H2 offers unique style and superior off-road performance, but it is not the most comfortable car for everyday driving. Consumers balance all of these factors and more when assessing the benefits of different vehicle choices. When it comes to most intangible benefits, different customers would place a different monetary value on each.

It is sufficient that consumers *perceive* that a product offers superior benefits, even if there is no tangible evidence of those benefits. This may explain why many participants in blind taste tests cannot tell any difference between Coke and RC Cola, yet most consumers prefer to have Coke on hand rather than RC. Coke's market dominance is evidence enough that it delivers more value than RC. It is futile to argue that consumers are somehow irrational; this conclusion is more likely a failure of the analyst to truly understand the basis for the consumer's choice. We will take for granted that consumers do, in fact, make the right choice, and that this reflects the underlying product benefits. We revisit this argument in Chapter 4, when we detail how to quantify benefits.

B Minus C

We are now ready to understand our proposition. It helps to introduce a bit of notation. Let B measure the benefits or happiness the product gives its customers (measured in monetary terms). B should also account for any *user costs*, which include, for example, the costs of acquiring the product, learning to use the product, storing the product, and disposing of the product. Once we account for user costs, we can think of B as the maximum amount that consumers would be *willing to pay* to purchase the product. Let C measure production costs. This includes the cost of all inputs that had to be sacrificed or used up in the production process of that good (also measured in monetary terms). This is the amount that cost accountants are supposed to report as the cost of goods sold.

The amount of value that a firm creates is equal to B–C (B minus C). To prove our proposition, we need one more variable. Let P stand for the price. We can now divide value, or B–C, into two components:

1. **B–P = the benefits enjoyed by consumers, above and beyond the purchase price.** Firms that offer the highest levels of B–P will enjoy the largest market shares.
2. **P–C = the seller's profit per unit sold.** Firms that offer the highest P–C will have the biggest unit profit margins.

It should now be obvious that if a firm offers higher B–C than its rivals, then it can set price so that it simultaneously (1) offers consumers more B–P than do competitors, and (2) enjoys a higher P–C than competitors. This translates into a larger market share, profit margins, and higher profits.

One important implication is that from the standpoint of a firm's strategy, *there is no such thing as a price position or a price advantage.* Any firm can set a low price, but if it does not have low costs, it will simply go out of business faster than its rivals. By the same token, any firm can set a high price, but without high benefits, it will have no customers and soon perish. Successful positioning requires creating B–C. Pricing is just the means used to translate that position into profits.

Firms that create high B–C do not have to aim for both a higher market share and higher margins at the same time. It might make more sense for a firm with a B–C advantage to increase its price to the point where it enjoys very high margins but a relatively small market share (think Neiman Marcus). There are other situations when it makes sense to keep prices low, resulting in a dominant share but with lower margins (think Wal-Mart). We detail the choice between a "margin strategy" and a "share strategy" later in this chapter.

CONNECTING GENERIC STRATEGIES AND B–C

In the books *Competitive Strategy* (1980) and *Competitive Advantage* (1985), Harvard Business School's Michael Porter argues that firms should choose among three generic positions or strategies ("cost advantage," "differentiation advantage," and "niche strategy").[2] These generic strategies are often a cornerstone of strategic analysis. While the B–C framework is an alternative to generic strategies, you need not unlearn the generic strategy approach. In Table 2.1, we see how the two approaches compare.

Cost advantage is analogous to reducing C across a broad product line, while maintaining reasonable B parity. Firms such as Hyundai and Saturn succeed in this way. Firms such as Kia have lower costs, but their B is so low that they have failed to win many customers.

Differentiation advantage stems from desirable characteristics that make a firm unique, such as Federal Express's reliability or Nordstrom's customer service. A differentiated firm is uniquely better on dimensions

Table 2.1
Porter's Generic Strategy Framework

Porter's Generic Strategy	B–C Analogue	Examples
Cost Advantage	Lower C; Comparable B	Dell Computer; Wal-Mart
Differentiation Advantage	Higher B; Comparable C	Cray, Inc. (Supercomputers); Nordstrom
Niche Strategy	Higher B–C in narrow market space	Gateway (home office market); Bed Bath & Beyond

that virtually all consumers prefer (as opposed to being better in ways that appeal to just a few consumers). This is analogous to increasing B in the eyes of most consumers.

A focus strategy is a cost or differentiation strategy that is limited to a submarket and may not appeal to most consumers. For example, the Martin-Brower Company is a global distribution services company that is the largest provider of supply chain management services to the McDonald's worldwide restaurant chain. These services include specialized distribution and extensive truck fleet operations. Because the firm is focused on a narrow customer base (mainly one customer!) the firm is able to generate higher benefits and/or is able to produce its services at lower costs relative to a firm configured to serve a greater variety of customers.

Focus strategies are especially attractive when competitors are pursuing broader cost or differentiation strategies that fail to deliver consistent B–C across all customer segments. Microsoft Word dominates the word processor software market, but does not deliver particularly high value to a number of customer segments. For example, many academic researchers need to type complex mathematical formulae, a task that is well beyond the capabilities of MS Word. This has created an opportunity for TCI Software Research, whose Scientific Word dominates this small but profitable market niche.

In addition to being a complementary means to express the firm's position, we think many analysts will find the B–C framework more flexible than the generic strategy approach. The B–C framework builds on the generic strategies by allowing us to think quantitatively about positioning. Positioning is more than just a trichotomous choice; firms are precisely positioned along a B–C spectrum. Viewing positioning along a continuum will aid in successful identification and implementation of strategy. This point is nicely illustrated by considering what happens to firms that are "stuck in the middle."

Stuck in the Middle

Many strategists, including Porter, admonish firms not to pursue more than one generic strategy at a time, lest they end up stuck in the middle, with neither a cost nor a differentiation advantage. There are many examples of firms that unsuccessfully straddle strategic options, making a compelling case for avoiding such apparent strategic indecision. However, by considering this argument in light of the B–C approach, we see that there is much more to the concept of "stuck in the middle" than a simple strategic rule of thumb.

The B–C framework does not imply a necessary tradeoff between strategic options. Consider the value creation strategies listed in Table 2.2. Firms can decrease C, increase B, or *do both*. The latter value creation strategy should be possible according to the B–C framework.

In fact, there are many examples of firms that appear to offer higher B *and* lower C than does the competition—lean-differentiators, if you will. Toyota and Honda revolutionized the market for small and mid-size family cars in the 1980s by offering better quality at lower prices. American Airlines seemed to occupy such a strategic position through the 1980s, before Southwest expanded and American's unions extracted large wage concessions. In these examples, firms improved their production technology (Toyota and Honda through total quality management, American through its revolutionary Sabre reservation system) and, as a result, enjoyed higher B and lower C.

There are many other examples of firms that succeed without offering either the highest B or lowest C, but simply by offering high B–C: Dannon yogurts, Panasonic DVD players, Dell computers, and Chrysler

Table 2.2
Stuck in the Middle Strategy

Value Creation Strategy	B–C Position	Porter Position
Achieve lowest cost position in industry.	Outcompete rival.	Cost advantage.
Achieve highest benefit position in industry.	Outcompete rival.	Benefit advantage.
Decrease C and increase B to achieve highest value position in industry.	Outcompete rival.	Stuck in the middle.

minivans are all market leaders that give consumers high value, but offer neither the highest B nor the lowest C. The facts clearly show that firms can succeed without having the highest B or the lowest C. Moreover, it would be foolish to advise Dell to abolish its customer service (reduce B by a lot, just to save a bit on C) or to tell Chrysler to build more powerful minivans that handle like sports cars (raise C a lot and B a little). These firms have found just the right balance of B and C; any movement would reduce their value creation.

Yet we do not wish to dismiss the potential problems of being stuck in the middle. If consumers have sufficiently differentiated preferences, then the firms that pursue value creation may end up offering high value to the small number of median consumers, leaving the bulk of the market to firms that focus on the high or low end.

We also suspect that firms get stuck in the middle because of problems with strategic implementation. When firms face the following conditions, clarity of strategic purpose may be valuable:

- Achieving cost or benefit excellence involves discontinuities. It is sometimes difficult to improve product quality without substantial investments. For example, it costs $500 million to develop a new heart drug; one cannot develop a heart drug that is half as good for $250 million. In these situations, compromise leads to disaster— vast sums spent with no benefit improvements to show for it. Discontinuities also characterize the world of entertainment, where one movie (or one recording) might be slightly better than the rest, yet command the lion's share of sales revenues.

- This problem is magnified if lower level managers have great discretion over resources. Managers who confront daily the tradeoffs that determine the success of corporate strategy may need unambiguous guidance from senior executives, or find it difficult to determine how to resolve them. If different managers commit to different objectives, and the firm cannot achieve any objectives through piecemeal measures, then success may again be elusive. We recommend that senior executives make the firm's objectives clear to all managers. It never hurts to create value, but if the firm seeks a specific position in the marketplace, be sure everyone knows where the firm is heading.

The bottom line is that "stuck in the middle" may have more to do with strategy implementation than with strategy selection. Firms that create the most value should outperform their rivals. But firms may prefer the simplicity of focusing on B or C to the complexity of weighing B against C, especially when there are discontinuities.

Disruptive Technologies

Another popular concept in strategy, *disruptive technologies*, fits nicely into the B–C framework. The term, which was coined by Harvard Business School's Clay Christensen, is used to describe new products that offer consumers low quality but are also much cheaper to produce than existing technologies. These products have the potential to fundamentally change the landscape of an industry. Honda's early motorcycle line (smaller engines than Harley's), personal computers (less powerful than mainframes), and e-mail (less personal than "snail mail") are among countless examples.

Using the Porter framework of benefit and cost advantage, it is easy to understand the threat posed by disruptive technologies. Firms with a benefit advantage ignore the new technology. In short order, the benefit leaders suffer irreparable harm as their market shares wither. This seems like a deep insight, combining an old theory (Porter's) with a novel idea (Christensen's) to reach new and profound conclusions.

The B–C framework reveals that there is actually nothing new or profound in the concept of disruptive technologies. In fact, it is just another example of the general concept that firms thrive by creating value. Remember that consumers do not care only about B; they care about B–P. With its dramatically lower C and somewhat lower B, a disruptive technology enables new firms to offer attractive B-P positions to even the most demanding customers, while still enjoying higher profit margins. The predictable result is that the firms with the highest B–C come to dominate the market.

Christensen observes that many disruptive technologies are "stealth technologies," in the sense that they often go unnoticed when first introduced, but catch on as the technology catches up. In effect, B improves over time, increasing the B–C differential in favor of the newcomer. But the observation that new technologies improve over time is true in general, not just for low B/lower C disruptive technologies. (As we discuss in Chapter 8, the learning curve is nearly ubiquitous.)

In the final analysis, the concept of disruptive technology is just a special application of B–C. Firms that are wedded to the pursuit of a benefit advantage—mistakenly believing that a high B is sufficient for success—will be surprised by a disruptive technology. But firms that pay attention to B–C will not.

THE TARGET

All firms have a natural or *target* customer segment. In B–C talk, the target segment is the particular set of customers for whom the firm generates the highest B–C. Either the target segment perceives the B of the firm's output to be high relative to the perception of other customers, or the target segment is less costly for the firm to serve relative to the cost of serving other customers. A target segment can be large (think of the customers attracted by Wal-Mart's low prices or Toyota's reliability) or small (only a select group of audiophiles would consider paying $10,000 for a Theta Digital home theater sound processor.) Using Porter's terminology, targeting is relevant to firms pursuing a niche strategy.

It is usually easy to see how a product generates B–C for its target segment. Breyer's Carb Smart line of ice creams generates B for customers who struggle to reconcile their love of ice cream with their desire to stay on the Atkins diet. Precor's folding treadmills target exercise fanatics with limited floor space. Apex Digital's low end DVD players target customers with small screen televisions who would not notice the improved quality of higher cost units.

Target identification is essential for positioning. Without it, firms will usually fail to provide an attractive level of B–C for any customer segment. If the firm's management sincerely believes that everyone should prefer the firm's product or even view it as equivalent to the offerings of competitors, it is likely (and unfortunate for the owners of the firm) that the firm's management has never explicitly performed target identification. In identifying their target, firms should not only isolate customers who perceive a higher B when consuming the firm's output, but also determine the cost differential of serving different customers. For example, managers of firms whose products are expensive to transport should know exactly how costs change with distance. Quite simply, thinking strategically about one's business means identifying the firm's target customer segment and truly committing to this definition.

Ted Williams became a baseball hitting legend as a player for the Boston Red Sox. Williams is famous for saying, "Get a good pitch to hit." Williams's hitting strategy is depicted in Figure 2.1. He divided his strike zone into 77 baseballs, 7 wide by 11 high. Williams projected what he would hit at each pitch location, from .230 on the low-outside strike to .400 in what he called his "happy zone," the heart of the plate, belt high.[3] Another of Williams's quotes, "All I want out of life is when I walk down the street people say 'There goes the greatest hitter that ever lived' " was realized in 1941, when Williams hit .406, making him the last baseball player to break the magic .400 barrier.

SWINGING ONLY AT YOUR TARGET

Anyone who aspires to be known as the "greatest manager who ever lived" would do well to take two lessons from Williams's approach to targeting:

1. *Find the customer base that falls in your "happy zone"*—the customers to whom you can deliver the most value.[4] Williams knew that he could not reach all pitches with equal effectiveness, so he studied statistics on his own performance to assess where he had the most success.

2. *Be disciplined.* Williams's thorough knowledge of the strike zone and willingness to lay off pitches out of his happy zone produced a nearly 3-to-1 ratio of walks to strikeouts, an unheard-of statistic for a power hitter. He fanned 64 times as a rookie, and never more than 54 in any other season. Similarly, it requires a tremendous amount of impulse control to resist "swinging" at customers who are on the "low outside."

Figure 2.1
Ted Williams's Happy Zone

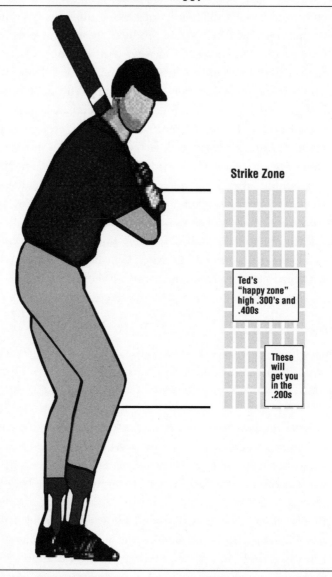

Strike Zone

Ted's "happy zone" high .300's and .400s

These will get you in the .200s

Ted Williams thought of the strike zone as a grid of 77 balls. He learned that choosing where to swing in the grid determined the hitter's batting average. Low and on the outside was least desirable, with the "happy zone" in the middle of the grid. Analogously, you can divide your customers into a grid, where your "batting average" is your profitability in serving a customer or customer segment. Ted would say, stick to your happy zone.

Most business managers understand that there are customers they should not serve. Yet those who have rigorously applied discipline to customer targeting are strictly in the minority. Few firms have the stomach to relinquish existing customers and identify customers whom they will *not* serve. But successful B–C analysis requires managers to assess value creation by customer segment, and stick to those segments for which the firm delivers superior B–C.

TARGETING SUPPLIERS

Most targeting efforts look at ways to increase B for specific customer segments. It is also possible to create value by targeting suppliers. Targeting suppliers creates value by reducing the costs of critical inputs—those inputs that have a large impact on unit costs.

To understand how to target suppliers, consider that the input suppliers to any one firm usually have outside options. Disney's animators have their choice of movie studios, Lucas Verity can sell its antilock brake components to its choice of car makers, and Boise Cascade can sell its wood to countless furniture makers. The amount that a firm has to pay an input supplier is almost entirely determined by the attractiveness of the supplier's outside options. Supplier targeting means identifying inputs whose outside options are unattractive relative to being employed by the firm in question. The firm will not have to pay these suppliers full market wages and will, as a result, hold down its costs.

The firm can enhance the power of supplier targeting by creating *targeted benefits*. Targeted benefits have two characteristics. First, *the target's valuation of these benefits should exceed the costs of creating them*. For example, suppose that a firm can give employees a flextime benefit valued at $15,000 per year, and that flextime costs the firm only $5,000 per employee per year. From the employee's point of view, flextime is like getting a $15,000 raise. The firm can now reduce wages by as much as $15,000 without losing the employee. This strategy works only if other firms do not also offer flextime; otherwise, competitors will bid up wages until the workers capture all the value for themselves. Thus, the second feature of targeted benefits is that *they are not likely to be offered by other firms*. If you have already targeted your suppliers correctly, then they have few outside options, and this second feature is automatically present.

Firms can offer a wide menu of valuable benefits to their suppliers, including technological expertise, reputation enhancement, income security, and even social connections. These may all lead to targeted benefits that allow the firm to reduce C. One caveat is in order. Targeted benefits may affect the mix of suppliers willing to work for the firm. That is, the benefit may result in a degree of self-selection among applicants. For example, flextime may be more appealing to individuals with children. The firm must determine the costs and benefits of this self-selection.

TACTICS FOR VALUE CREATION

The tactics firms use to create B–C vary by industry. But they tend to fall into a small number of generic categories. Table 2.3 presents a laundry list of value creation tactics. As we emphasize in the next chapter, the most effective tactics are those that are most difficult to imitate. In addition to listing tactics, we offer comments about how likely it is that other firms can imitate them. Those that are hardest to imitate are the best sources of an enduring positioning advantage.

CHOOSING P TO OPTIMALLY EXPLOIT B–C

A firm with higher B–C than its rivals can surely outperform them. If all consumers were identical, that firm could quickly enjoy a monopoly. Here is how:

- If the firm has lower C and comparable B, it can set its price to just below its rivals' costs. For the competitors to remain in the market, they would have to lose money on every sale. More likely than not, the competition will soon exit. This actually occurs in some commodity markets such as chemicals, where a company obtains a patent on a new production process, reduces its production costs, and prices the competition out of the market.

Table 2.3
Value Creation Tactics

Options to Reduce C	Examples of Action	Comments
Drive cost reductions through product market activities.	• "Buy" share in existing markets through low prices to increase scale. • "Buy" share in existing markets to accumulate experience. • Introduce new products to better utilize shared facilities. • Enter new geographies to improve capacity utilization or increase scale.	*Easy for competitors to imitate, but may create positional or early-mover advantages; being first is often key.*
Control cost drivers within the firm's activities.	• Reallocation of production within existing facilities. • Relocation of facilities to low input-cost regions. • Input substitution (e.g., for labor). • Use lower-cost components. • Special terms or "trades" with key suppliers. • Enhance worker productivity through incentive systems. • Outsource major cost centers. • Reductions in work force.	*Not that difficult for competitors to imitate.*
	• Use of nonmonetary compensation. • Improve material yields. • Reduce complexity of production operations (e.g., reduce SKUs). • Alterations in product design to improve manufacturability. • Push improvements in asset management (i.e., lower inventories). • Enhance worker productivity through changes in organizational structure.	*More difficult for competitors to imitate.*

(Continued)

Table 2.3 *(Continued)*

Options to Reduce C	Examples of Action	Comments
Dramatically reconfigure firm's value chain.	• Major re-engineering initiatives.	*Available to all but hard to do well.*

Options to Improve B	Examples of Action	Comments
Enhance physical characteristics of the product.	• Add features. • Improve aesthetics. • Enhance performance. • Enhance durability. • Reduce defect rates.	*Simple product changes are easy to imitate. Enduring improvements are easy to aim for but often hard to reach.*
Bundle complementary products or services.	• Warranties/service contracts. • Spare parts. • Quality presale technical advice/training. • Postsale consulting services.	*Opportunities to exploit competencies in complementary markets. Raises question of whether firm should focus in the complementary market, however.*
Enhance sale or delivery of good/reduce buyer purchase costs.	• Firm location. • Product-line extension for "one-stop" shopping. • Availability/generosity of trade credit. • Easy order-placing. • Speed/timeliness of delivery.	*Location is a unique asset.* *One-stop shopping requires scale and scope.* *Firms can develop competencies in order fulfillment.*
Improve product image.	• Compelling packaging/labeling. • Compelling advertising messages.	*Neither is predictable and neither is predictably unique.*
Create uniqueness in drastically different ways.	• Paradigm-breaking new product concepts.	*Competency in R&D can lead to a lasting advantage.*

• If the firm has higher B and comparable C, it can raise its price to equal the sum of its rivals' costs plus the benefit differential. For competitors to stay in the market, they will have to cut their own prices below costs; otherwise, consumers will get a better deal from the high P/higher B firm. Again, competitors will likely exit. This does not occur as often as the first scenario, because markets in which there are opportunities to increase B are usually characterized by product differentiation.

Exploiting B–C in Differentiated Goods Markets

In many markets, consumers disagree about which products represent the best buys. This means that the products are differentiated. (We have a lot more to say about differentiation later on in the book.) Automobiles provide a quintessential example of differentiation. Most everyone agrees that Honda offers higher B than Hyundai, but some consumers purchase Hyundais. This is because consumers do not put the same dollar value on each car's benefits. Consider that the Honda Accord currently sells for about $22,000, a comparably equipped Hyundai Sonata for about $18,000. Some consumers believe the Honda's higher B is worth $4,000; others disagree.

It does not have to be this way. Honda could lower its prices to be comparable to Hyundai. Honda would then gain market share but make a much smaller profit margin per vehicle. This suggests the dilemma faced by all firms that enjoy a B–C advantage in differentiated goods markets: Should they take the profits in the form of higher market share or higher margins? The answer depends on whether the firm's advantage comes from a higher B or lower C, as well as the price sensitivity of consumers.

Honda accounts for both of these factors when setting prices. Honda enjoys a clear B advantage over Hyundai, while also realizing near C parity. (Honda's scale and experience allow it to keep costs near the levels of the cost leading South Korean firms.) Suppose that Honda believes that its customers are very price sensitive. Then it would make sense to lower its price on the Accord to somewhere near $18,000 and enjoy a big increase in market share. Honda has not sought price parity, however, preferring to maintain a 20 percent price premium. The reason is that many Honda buyers are quite loyal and will not switch to Hyundai, even to save $4,000. Honda is better off enjoying large margins and solid market share, rather than small margins and slightly higher shares.

Table 2.4 summarizes whether sellers of differentiated goods should exploit their B–C advantage through higher market shares or higher margins, depending on the price sensitivity of consumers.

WRAP-UP: THE ADVANTAGES OF THE B–C FRAMEWORK

The B–C framework offers several advantages over other frameworks for strategy. Perhaps the most important is that it is grounded in economic theory. There is an unbroken chain of logic from the economics of supply and demand to the strategic importance of B–C. Another advantage is that B–C helps to unify seemingly different strategic con-

Table 2.4
Exploiting a Competitive Advantage through Pricing

	Cost Advantage	*Benefit Advantage*
High consumer price sensitivity	• Modest price cuts gain lots of market share, so choose. *Share Strategy* Underprice competitors to gain share.	• Modest price hikes lose lots of market share, so choose. *Share Strategy* Maintain price parity and let benefit advantage drive share increases.
Low consumer price sensitivity	• Big price cuts gain little share, so choose. *Margin Strategy* Maintain price parity and let lower costs drive higher margins.	• Big price hikes lose little share, so choose. *Margin Strategy* Charge price premium relative to competitors.

cepts, including Porter's positioning strategies, stuck in the middle, and disruptive technologies. Finally, the B–C framework provides valuable insights into tactical decisions such as pricing. We return to the simple concept of B–C throughout the book.

NOTES

1. That is, think of costs in the traditional economic sense: the direct and indirect (opportunity cost) of the resources used to produce the firm's output. The opportunity cost portion is roughly the book value of the firm's productive capital multiplied by the firm's cost of capital.

2. M. E. Porter, *Competitive Strategy: Techniques for Analyzing Industries and Competitors,* New York: Free Press, 1980. (Republished with a new introduction, 1998.) M. E. Porter, *Competitive Advantage: Creating and Sustaining Superior Performance,* New York: Free Press, 1985. (Republished with a new introduction, 1998.)

3. Ted Williams and John Underwood, *The Science of Hitting,* New York: Fireside, 1986.

4. The CEO of Oil-Dri Corporation, Dan Jaffee, shared this analogy with the authors.

CHAPTER 3

AFFIRMING YOUR COMPETITIVE ADVANTAGE: THE RESOURCES AND CAPABILITIES AUDIT

Looking down at the corporate landscape from 40,000 feet, it is easy to identify the firms that create the most B–C. More likely than not, they are the ones generating the highest profits. Here are some examples. Avon Products sells directly to customers in their homes, making cosmetics shopping fun and convenient. By increasing B in this unique way, Avon is routinely ranked as one of the most profitable companies in America. eBay is the busiest marketplace in the world, giving buyers access to millions of sellers and sellers access to millions of buyers. The result is higher B, lower C, and among the best returns of any company in the new economy. Another hi-tech winner, Dell Computer, keeps inventory costs to a bare minimum through its just-in-time production techniques. The resulting low C (and a high perceived B) has helped make Michael Dell one of the wealthiest people in the world.

We ought to be skeptical any time we come across a firm that seems unable to generate superior B–C yet reports high profits. Neither HealthSouth, WorldCom, nor Enron pursued strategies destined to generate more B–C than their rivals; eventually, their accounting data caught up with the realities of their weak strategic positions.

Down on the ground, sorting out the winners and losers is more challenging. Accounting data—especially measures such as economic value added—are usually informative, the Enrons of the world notwith-standing. But while accounting data can tell us whether firms are prof-itable, they do not tell us how or why, or whether success might be fleeting. Enduring success comes from superior B–C; accounting data merely reflect that success. How can a firm assess whether it is creating more B–C than its rivals? How can the firm determine if it can protect its advantage? And how can it be sure that B–C will translate into prof-its? The *resource-based view of the firm* helps answer these questions.

The resource-based view (RBV) builds on a familiar idea in strategy: Firms must possess *resources* and *capabilities* to be successful. Think of re-sources as nouns—the things a firm possesses that allow it to prosper. According to the RBV, differences in the profits of competing firms are often attributable to differences in the bundles of resources they depend upon to make and sell their products. Firms with superior resources can produce their output more efficiently than their rivals and/or they can deliver more consumer benefits than their rivals.

It is often easy to identify the key resources of successful organiza-tions. Avon Products has a broad line of good quality cosmetics and a team of loyal, even fanatical salespeople who have close relationships with their customers. eBay has a patented auction technology and a large installed base of buyers and sellers. Dell has an inventory manage-ment expertise that is second to none in the industry, and a highly knowledgeable and courteous technical support staff.

However, resources alone do not guarantee success. Firms must apply their resources to create B–C. Think of capabilities as verbs—describing what the firm does with its resources. Avon Products makes shopping fun. eBay makes shopping and selling fun and assures all participants of the best possible prices. Dell can assemble personal computers faster and at lower cost than anyone else. Dell also provides outstanding telephone customer service. Table 3.1 summarizes the distinction between re-sources and capabilities.

Every firm should be able to list its resources and capabilities. But the resource-based view has a lot more to offer than simply reaffirming the strategist's mantra about the need to do things well. The most important insight of the RBV is that resources and capabilities are not profitable in and of themselves. The RBV identifies two conditions—*scarcity* and *im-*

Table 3.1
Resources and Capabilities

Resources	Nouns—things the firm possesses	Examples: Patents, talented workforce, brand name, location
Capabilities	Verbs—things the firm does well	Examples: Produce efficiently, offer good customer service, customize orders

mobility—under which resources and capabilities translate into profits. The RBV identifies one more condition that we call *scopability* that enables the firm to leverage scarce, immobile resources and capabilities for long-term growth and profits. We discuss all three conditions and then provide a tool for assessing a firm's strategic position under the RBV: the *Resources and Capabilities Audit*.

SCARCITY

One of the fundamental tenets of the RBV is that a firm cannot outperform its rivals unless its resources and capabilities are *scarce*. By keeping this in mind, it is often possible to reject some popular misconceptions about why firms succeed while honing in on the real reasons for their success. Consider the countless students of business strategy who have pondered why Southwest Airlines succeeded when older and larger carriers struggled. Many students credit much of the success of Southwest Airlines to the esprit de corps of its flight attendants. Fly Southwest and you are treated like a friend and neighbor by the cheeriest flight attendants in the skies; fly another carrier and expect indifference at best, churlishness at worst.

There is some truth to this argument; passengers routinely report that Southwest provides a cheerful in-flight experience. (Well, that is a bit of an oxymoron, but you get the point.) But we doubt whether cheerfulness is really the source of Southwest's success. Did Southwest corner the nation's supply of upbeat workers? Do United and American hire sourpusses? Of course not.

Fortunately, cheerfulness is not scarce, and no firm can corner the market on good vibes. So why do Southwest's customers give the carrier such high marks? The idea that Southwest's flight attendants are cheerier is part myth: There are many cheerful flight attendants on all carriers. But it is also the case that Southwest's business model, with service to smaller and less congested airports, fewer delays, and fewer lost bags makes for a happier flying experience for passengers and employees alike. It is also true that Southwest makes a special emphasis to screen employees for attitude, whereas other carriers may care more about experience or other worker attributes. As we discuss in Chapter 9, the reasons for Southwest's sustained success run far deeper than its esprit de corps.

Along the same lines, we have heard more than a few MBA students ascribe part of Wal-Mart's success to its door greeters. ("Hi, welcome to Wal-Mart!") The RBV rejects out-of-hand the theory that door greeters contribute to superior performance. There is an abundant supply of jolly souls willing to greet customers at K-Mart and Sears. Either K-Mart and Sears are too stupid/stubborn to hire them, or door greeters are not that important. The stupid/stubborn explanation seems unlikely, especially since K-Mart and Sears have had decades to mull it over and even employ a few cheerful greeters in selected stores. The door greeters may be a nice touch, but explain little, if any, of Wal-Mart's success, which has much more to do with its inventory controls and order processing capabilities. K-Mart and Sears have been unable to copy these capabilities,[1] and their financial results suffer accordingly.

More on Scarcity

There are more subtle and important examples of scarcity. Consider a classic question facing many pharmaceutical firms: Should they stake their success on developing capabilities in sales or in R&D? Pharmaceutical companies spend millions of dollars annually selling their products, and rightfully so. Sales efforts can make or break a drug in a crowded therapeutic category. But selling skills are not scarce, and no pharmaceutical company should base its future on a core competence in sales. If you don't believe this claim, consider the following facts and thought experiment.

Here are the facts. GlaxoSmithKline, whose depression medication Paxil and anxiety remedy Wellbutrin help the company to over $25 billion in annual drug sales, is one of the three largest firms in the industry. Schering Plough has one solid seller (Claritin) and only about $8 billion in annual drug sales. Glaxo not only outsells Schering, it has four times the market capitalization. Glaxo is clearly the superior performer. The question is why? Does Glaxo possess a superior sales force, or is there some other reason?

Here is the thought experiment. Suppose Glaxo and Schering swapped their patents. What do you suppose would happen to revenues at the two companies?

If sales were the key to success, then Glaxo would remain one of the top three pharmaceutical companies and Schering would remain mired in mediocrity, even if they swapped patents. But when we pose this hypothetical to pharmaceutical sales executives, they tell us that Glaxo's sales force would be hard pressed to boost sales much above Schering's preswap levels. At the same time, there is little doubt that Schering's sales force would do a terrific job selling Glaxo's present stable of products (and Schering would undoubtedly expand its sales force in the process). Make no mistake, Glaxo does a terrific job of selling its innovations. But so does Schering. That is the point; selling skills are not scarce. Glaxo outperforms Schering because it has more and better drugs to sell, which itself is a reflection of Glaxo's superior patents. Glaxo's patents are the scarce resources that make it successful.[2]

The pharmaceutical industry has recently experienced an epidemic of mergers, motivated in part by a desire to increase research productivity. But there is almost no evidence to support a link between company size and R&D success in the industry. In fact, many of the most important new innovations come from boutique research companies and from universities. If mergers are meant to improve R&D, we believe the strategy is misguided.

Even if mergers do facilitate R&D, merger implementation is never easy and can doom the best laid plans. When Pharmacia and Upjohn merged in 1995, they expected that doubling the scale of their research enterprise would lead to more drugs in the pipeline. Unfortunately, when CEO John Zabriskie tried to export many of Upjohn's centralized personnel practices to Pharmacia's decentralized research staff, the Pharmacia researchers balked and R&D productivity nosedived. It took a new CEO and new personnel practices before research productivity was restored to premerger levels. This reminds us that the strategy process is not complete until the strategy has been successfully executed.

Another example of a scarce resource comes from the broadcast network industry. Many pundits predicted that the major broadcast networks (ABC, NBC, CBS, and FOX) would be severely harmed by cable networks (ESPN, CNN), whose unique and often high quality programs would siphon away viewers and erode ad revenues. Cable networks have harmed the networks for sure, but nowhere near the extent forecasted by industry naysayers. This raises the question: What is the scarce resource that networks have but cable channels do not? The answer is access to a large, diverse audience.

Advertisers are often interested in having their message heard at once by a large audience made up of a variety of potential customers. Most cable content targets specific customer segments, and the general interest cable channels like HBO require extra fees, so they are not picked up by most households. Hence, even though the number of viewers of broadcast network programming has declined, the networks still control access to the kind of diverse audiences prized by advertisers. This allows the networks to command a far higher "price per eyeball" for their advertising slots relative to the prices charged by the cable networks.

IMMOBILITY

If a firm wants to convert its resources and capabilities into profits, then scarcity alone is not enough. The firm must have either actual or *de facto* ownership of the valuable resources, or else the real owner will reap the profits. Using RBV terminology, the firm's resources and capabilities must be *immobile*.

Resources and capabilities are immobile if (1) they cannot be bought and sold in the marketplace without the firm's permission, or (2) if the resource can be bought and sold, there is no other firm that can use the resource as productively. Taken together, these requirements imply that the resources and capabilities that make a firm successful cannot be taken from the firm and sold to a higher bidder. The concept of immobility helps explain why consumer products firms such as Coca-Cola and Anheuser-Busch sustain success for so long. Their main resources are their brands, which are inexorably tied to the firms. The concept also explains why popular restaurants often go out of business. Their main resource is often their location, which they do not usually own. A savvy landlord keeps rents just low enough to make sure the space is occupied, but not so low as to leave much profit on the table for the restaurateur.

If one firm's asset can be used by another (without the permission of the first), then it is a mobile asset. This sounds simple enough, yet positioning analyses often fail to consider mobility. There are also several subtleties to the concept of mobility, which we now discuss.

Mobility Issues

Many firms mistakenly stake their future on mobile assets. For years, Foot Locker has been the place to buy Nike athletic shoes. At the same time, Nike was Foot Locker's best selling brand. In 2002, Foot Locker focused on less expensive shoes, cutting orders of Nike's marquee products by $250 million. Nike played hardball, curtailing shipments to Foot Locker by an additional $150 million. Foot Locker held firm, convinced it could keep its customers by selling more Reeboks, K-Swiss, and other brands. Nike was equally sure that it could hold its own by selling more shoes through other retailers. The next 12 months would demonstrate that these firms needed each other more than they would admit.

Both firms thought they held the more potent asset. Foot Locker believed its customers valued its locations and knowledgeable staff; Nike was confident in the power of its brand. While Nike and Foot Locker put on brave faces during their dispute, reality hit hard. Foot Locker experienced small but steady declines in same store sales. Nike's U.S. shoe sales fell by as much as 10 percent, and profits fell by half. By July 2003, the two had patched things up, having realized that neither firm could enjoy the same level of profits without partnering with the other. They were soon developing exclusive joint marketing programs. They have picked up the pieces and, a bit scarred, moved on from the battle.

The Gap stores once had a similar relationship with Levi's jeans. Together, the Gap and Levi's prospered. The Gap eventually introduced an eponymous line of jeans and jettisoned the Levi's brand altogether. The Gap's main asset was no longer mobile and the Gap enjoyed two decades of rising profits while Levi's struggled. In a move made partly out of desperation, Levi's has agreed to overhaul its production and distribution practices to meet Wal-Mart's strict standards. Levi's hopes that its brand name still has enough leverage that, when combined with Wal-Mart's access to customers, it can enjoy a corporate revival.

The key lesson is that you must not only identify the resources and capabilities that make your firm successful, but also be honest about who owns these assets. To the owner go the spoils.

Most of the time, workers are mobile. For years, the partners of the famous New York law firm Cravath, Swaine & Moore benefited handsomely from the highly profitable practice of partner and superstar trial lawyer David Boies. In 1997, Boies left Cravath and set up his own firm, Boies, Schiller & Flexner. When he left Cravath, he took his profits with him. Stories like these are not unusual; even academia has a few. It is not uncommon for superstar researchers capable of bringing in millions of dollars in grants to shop themselves around to the highest bidding university. In addition to commanding large salaries, these scholars get their own multimillion-dollar research facilities.

Some of the best known examples of the mobility of superstars come from motion pictures and television, where the producers of popular content and their suppliers tend to expropriate much of what would accrue to the networks as profits. Consider the $1 billion annual fee that ESPN is paying the National Football League to show Monday Night Football.

The Winner's Curse

Many firms try to buy scarce, valuable assets from others. They buy other firms' patents and brands and may even buy other firms in their entirety. This is rarely a formula for success. Owners of scarce, valuable assets are usually not stupid (or they would be hard pressed to develop such assets in the first place). They would only sell their assets at a price that is at least equal to the discounted sum of all future profits the asset would generate. At such a price, the acquirer can do no better than break even on the deal, unless the acquirer can find a better, more productive use for the asset.[3] Even so, many firms pursue scarce assets. They must believe they can wring more profits out of them. Perhaps they are right. But empirical evidence suggests that instead of turning a profit, they are more likely to succumb to the Winner's Curse.

The Winner's Curse looms whenever more than one bidder seeks an object that would be of roughly equal value to each of them. Bidding for offshore oil tracts, rare coins, and star athletes all create opportunities for the Winner's Curse. In these bidding situations, the firm that is most optimistic about the value of the asset usually makes the highest bid. Unfortunately, the firm that is most optimistic is often overoptimistic, causing it to bid too much. There is a lot of solid research evidence documenting the effects of the Winner's Curse on unwary bidders. For example, we know that firms systematically lose money when they acquire unrelated target companies. Overoptimism about potential synergies leads to overbidding.

Even experienced combatants like Coke and Pepsi have gotten caught up in the competition to acquire scarce assets. Beginning in 1996, Pepsi agreed to pay Pennsylvania State University $1.4 million annually in exchange for exclusive rights to sell and market Pepsi on the campus. Soon thereafter, Coke struck a similar deal with Rutgers University. Today, the two cola giants collectively pay about $100 million annually in exchange for exclusive rights to sell on college campuses, beaches, and other properties. It is not clear if either firm has gained anything from the Balkanization of the cola market; they are merely paying for a scarce asset (access to specific locations) that used to be free.

MOBILITY AND COSPECIALIZED ASSETS

If firms lose profits when their assets are mobile, then they can improve their position by reducing asset mobility. Consider the case of a management consulting firm. Most consulting firms are dependent on human capital to produce their output. How do consulting firms make sure that the owners of the human capital (i.e., the consultants) do not extract all the profits for themselves (as did David Boies)? The key is to make the consultants more productive if they remain in the firm than if they go to work elsewhere. Here is an example of how this can work.

Suppose that Alex the consultant brings in $300,000 of profits into his firm. Alex believes that his salary of $100,000 is low relative to his value to the firm, and wonders if he would be able to pocket the $300,000 if he worked on his own. Alex's manager, Sharon, needs to convince him that $100,000 is, in fact, more than fair. To do this, Sharon needs to make the case that the $300,000 is a result of Alex combining with the assets of the firm and that Alex on his own would generate a much lower profit.

Sharon should approach this argument in a well organized way. First, let's concentrate on Alex's top line—his revenues. Sharon could point out that Alex would have a harder time on his own attracting business—a prestigious firm has name recognition—Alex on his own does not. Furthermore, the advice from a prestigious firm is often more readily accepted by the client and the client's board of directors. Sharon could also suggest to Alex that the quality of his work would suffer if he did not have access to the other consultants or the firm's rich database of information (the firm's knowledge infrastructure). In brief, she needs to convince Alex that he would not earn nearly as much in revenues on his own. Then Sharon could discuss the cost side of the equation. She could point out that if he stays in the firm, Alex could benefit from economies of scale that result from costs being spread across many, many projects.

By carefully describing the $300,000 as a product of Alex's cospecialization with assets owned by the prestigious consulting firm, Sharon has shown Alex that his value outside the firm is considerably less than $300,000. While Alex is smart, has accumulated specialized skills valuable to the firm, and even has relationships with the firm's clients that are of value, he does not have the leverage to demand a salary of nearly $300,000.

But might Alex not just go to another consulting firm? Here again, we see some mechanisms at consulting firms that inhibit aggressive bidding for the Alexes of the world. First, these firms are careful not to develop a dependency on human resources that are too scarce. By hiring from a wide pool of MBAs and using training, very experienced managers, and a knowledge infrastructure (that is, a database that contains information about the firm's past engagements) to support them, consulting firms get high quality output without dependence on a very scarce resource.

We also observe that wages across consulting firms are quite comparable; consulting firms have disciplined themselves to avoid competing up the cost of their best consultants. Better to forgo a few good consultants than to break with the precedent of avoiding a lot of individual deals. (We have more to say about such competitive discipline in Chapters 5 and 6.) Keep in mind that this example is rather stylized; there are many superstar consultants, and they do command premium compensation.

Our example of Alex and Sharon points to three essential steps that any firm should take to capture the profits of erstwhile mobile assets:

1. Avoid dependency on scarce professional talent.
2. Tie workers to the firms by offering complementary resources: Create cospecialized assets.
3. Avoid intense competition to retain human capital. The latter step may require much of the same discipline required to avoid price wars, a topic we cover at length in Chapters 5 and 6.

The leverage of asset owners is based on relative bargaining power, and bargaining power can be engineered. The National Collegiate Athletic Association (NCAA) has taken full advantage of cospecialized assets in the production of college basketball games. Through its "March Madness" college basketball tournament, the NCAA has created a highly prized asset worth billions in television contract revenues. Many complain that college basketball players should enjoy a large cut of the revenues; after all, without the athletes there would be no games. But the athletes have no leverage. Only a few can play professional basketball, and fans tune in to the tournament regardless of which individual athletes are playing. The athletes depend entirely on the NCAA for their productivity. As long as the NCAA owns the rights to the tournament, it will reap the benefits of the work supplied by the cospecialized players.[4]

Productive work teams are an important source of cospecialization. Often, team members enhance each other's productivity in ways that could not be duplicated if they split apart or were replaced by outsiders. National Basketball Association (NBA) stars John Stockton and Karl Malone experienced firsthand the drawbacks of being cospecialized assets. Stockton and Malone played together for 18 years developing a rapport that is rare in professional sports. Their skills made the Utah Jazz one of the best teams of the 1990s, yet they were not among the highest paid players in the league. The reason appears to be that their contracts never expired at the same time, making it impossible for them to jointly sell their services to another team. No team wanted Stockton without Malone (or vice versa), so no team was willing to bid up either one's contract. John Stockton retired in 2003 and Karl Malone signed a (relatively) low salary contract to play with the Los Angeles Lakers. Malone's productivity declined precipitously. Some analysts thought he had gotten too old, while others wondered if he was neglected on a team that featured Kobe Bryant and Shaquille O'Neal. But every expert agreed that Malone looked lost without Stockton.

We can learn a lot from these sports stories. Make your asset the reason people buy the product. And if you must rely on assets owned by others, create processes that tie them together, for example by creating work teams. The ability to organize assets into teams is itself an asset and may be the scarcest of them all.

Scarcity and Cospecialization

We have argued that resources must be scarce to be a source of advantage. Thus, a firm could not expect to prosper by bidding for a valuable but scarce input (such as a superstar attorney). Competition from other bidders drives up the purchase price so that the owner of the scarce resource collects all the profits. This argument breaks down—and the leverage of scarce assets falls—if the firm's resources and capabilities are cospecialized with the scarce input. This is because the firm can make more out of the input than can any of its rivals. If the asset generates value of, say, $1,000 when used by a rival, then the rivals will bid no more than $1,000 to obtain it. The firm can bid $1,001, get the asset, and thanks to cospecialization, generate more than $1,001 in additional revenues.

During its remarkable growth in the 1980s, Microsoft enjoyed exactly this kind of benefit as it competed to hire the best software developers. Bill Gates commented that Microsoft's competition in the labor market was not with other computer firms, but with investment banking firms like Morgan Stanley Dean Witter. The reason: Microsoft wanted to hire people with the highest IQs, and Wall Street was becoming a magnet for many technical whizzes. But Microsoft offered these geniuses technical and business opportunities they could not get anywhere else, including Wall Street. As a result, Microsoft was able to attract the best and brightest without paying Wall Street wages.[5]

SCOPABLE ASSETS

Scarce and immobile resources and capabilities can deliver profits. If resources and capabilities are *scopable*—that is, they can be applied to new products and new geographic markets—then so much the better. As before, we rely on a few examples to illustrate some key principles. Think of Ray Kroc's excitement when he saw the popularity of the first McDonald's hamburgers stand in 1954. It took little imagination for him to reproduce that success in Chicagoland and nationwide. McDonald's was scopable for three reasons:

1. There were *untapped markets* for the product.
2. The production process was *easily reproduced*.
3. It had *unlimited access to capital*, in the form of franchisees.

These three features characterize most scopable resources and capabilities.

Diversifying into New Markets

Many factors create opportunities for firms to expand beyond their traditional territorial borders. Tariffs, capital markets, technology, legal and political infrastructure, demographics, and tastes all change over time, affecting the ability and desirability of firms to reach consumers. There is no better example than McDonald's. After conquering the United States, McDonald's continued to expand, and now is the world's leading food service retailer with more than 30,000 restaurants in 119 countries serving 46 million customers each day. McDonald's has learned how to work with virtually every form of economic system, and took advantage of the fall of communist Eastern Europe by finding willing franchisees and sources of meat, fish, and other key supplies. Beer makers have pursued similar global expansion strategies. However, firms such as Anheuser-Busch have learned that entering markets with foreign brands can cause intensely nationalistic feelings of rage and the entry to fail. Hence, some basic market research goes a long way toward identifying such opportunities for geographic diversification.

Firms can also scope their resources and capabilities by leveraging them into related businesses. In the course of obtaining regulatory approval for their new drugs, pharmaceutical companies have compiled literally truckloads of data on alternative treatments and outcomes. They now use these data to develop treatment guidelines used by hospitals, doctors, and managed care organizations to hold down costs while assuring high quality care.

Scoping the Production Process

Ray Kroc understood that anyone could learn how to make a McDonald's hamburger. All McDonald's franchises follow a highly regimented production process. There is no equivalent of McDonald's in high-end dining. When it comes to the world's greatest restaurants—Alain Ducasse in Paris or Charlie Trotter's in Chicago—the key resource is the executive chef. Executive chefs are not easily scopable. They may find time to write a cookbook or two, and maybe even to help create themes and menus at several restaurants. But they can only be in one kitchen. When gourmet chefs do open new restaurants, they often fail. When success does come, it is either because the chef has been able to train an equally brilliant sous chef as a replacement, or because the chef has invented a new style of dining that can be taught to others (a la

Wolfgang Puck's California cuisine). The bottom line: Unique assets are difficult to scope.

Access to Capital

It is nice to believe that anyone with a good scopable idea will find the financing to help it grow. The reality is that more people believe their ideas are scopable than there are scopable ideas, and banks will not finance anyone who asks. Ray Kroc grew not by relying on banks, but by relying on other entrepreneurs. He sold franchise rights, allowing others to operate their own McDonald's, in exchange for a variety of fees. Not only did this generate the capital for expansion, it assured that each store would be locally controlled, guaranteeing a level of service that could not be achieved by a centralized organization.

As a reminder, here are the three keys to scopability:

1. There are new markets for the good.
2. The production process is easily reproduced.
3. There is easy access to capital.

Scopability of Organizational Practices and Strategic Fit

Two or more products and services are scopable—in economics parlance, they enjoy economies of scope—when producing one makes it less costly to produce the other. A firm's organizational activities can also generate economies of scope—or what economists call *complementarities*—whenever the pursuit of one activity can enhance the efficiency of others. For example, Southwest Airlines strives for the fastest turnaround of any airline, often landing a plane and getting it ready for the next takeoff in less than 30 minutes. To do this, Southwest uses several complementary practices. It does not cater its flights. It uses a single type of plane (Boeing 737), thereby simplifying baggage handling, refueling, and maintenance procedures. It does not fly into congested airports. Each of these practices makes the others more effective, by eliminating potential bottlenecks.

The concept of complementarities is better known in the strategy literature as *strategic fit*. Strategic fit among organizational processes can be essential to firms seeking a long-term competitive advantage. Through a strong strategic fit, the whole of a firm's strategy exceeds the sum of the parts of its processes. (In a sense, strategic fit is to strategy what cospecialization is to assets.) Moreover, a good strategic fit can be difficult to imitate. Firms cannot simply copy one process at a time; they would have to copy them all at once. For example, United Airlines has recently launched Ted, a low-fare carrier intended to compete head on with Southwest. United can match Southwest on wages and other supply costs. It could even switch to a single type of plane and stop onboard catering, but unless it moves out of its congested Chicago hub and other crowded airports, it cannot hope to match Southwest's operational efficiencies.

THE RESOURCES AND CAPABILITIES AUDIT

As part of its strategic positioning analysis, every firm should perform a *resources and capabilities (R&C) audit*. This audit forces the firm to systematically think about each resource and capability. Is it really scarce? Is it truly immobile? If the answer to either question is no, then the resource or capability cannot be a source of enduring advantage. If it is scarce and immobile, the firm should determine if it is also scopable. If it is, then the resource or capability can help the firm grow.

Here is how to perform the R&C audit.

1. List your firm's resources and capabilities, using a template like Table 3.2. This step should be familiar to most managers who have been even remotely involved in strategic planning, as it is the *S* of SWOT analysis.
2. Assess the scarcity and mobility of each resource and capability.
3. If a resource is scarce and immobile, then also assess its scopability.
4. Whenever possible, square your audit with available facts.
5. Because you will want to discuss and debate your audit with others, be sure to provide annotations, providing the justification to any controversial claims.

Table 3.2
Resources and Capabilities Audit

Resource/ Capability	Is It Scarce?	Is It Mobile?	Is It Scopable?	Is It a Source of Enduring Advantage?

Let's see how an R&C audit might have warned Walt Disney Studios of a major strategic problem that emerged in the mid-1990s.

R&C AUDIT APPLICATION: DISNEY'S WALT DISNEY STUDIOS

In the summer of 1994, Disney's animated motion picture division, Walt Disney Studios, released *The Lion King*. It shattered every box office record—for both animated and live action films—and seemingly every child in the United States had a *Lion King*–themed birthday party. The theme song, "The Circle of Life," rode the pop charts and earned Elton John an Academy Award nomination, as did the songs "Hakuna Matata" and "Can You Feel the Love Tonight?" (the latter was the Oscar-winning song). The success of *The Lion King* capped a phenomenal six-year stretch, during which four Disney animated films (the others were *The Little Mermaid, Beauty and the Beast*, and *Aladdin*) enjoyed box office supremacy.

Other movie studios noticed Disney's success and released animated movies of their own. None succeeded. In 1992, the same year that *Aladdin* was pulling in hundreds of millions at the box office for Disney, Fox Studios released *Ferngully*. It managed just $33 million. Fox's 1993 release, *Once Upon a Forest*, did not even reach $9 million. What were Disney's resources and capabilities that enabled it to completely blow away its competition in the animated motion picture marketplace?

It is not difficult to generate the following R&C audit (Table 3.3) for Disney, circa 1994. If this R&C audit is correct, then Disney's animation skills and marketing team cannot explain its dominance, as neither asset was completely scarce or immobile. Disney's success, it seems, rested on the power of the Disney brand.

Squaring the Theory with the Facts

The audit provides a plausible theory, namely that Disney's extraordinary success in the animated motion picture industry was due largely to its brand name. Many industry analysts have offered the same argument. Unfortunately, this theory does not square with data on the economic performance of the Walt Disney Studios.

As we discussed in Chapter 1, a good strategy should be grounded in

Table 3.3
Disney R&C Audit

Resource/ Capability	Is It Scarce?	Is It Mobile?	Is It Scopable?	Is It a Source of Enduring Advantage?
The Disney brand	Yes	No	Yes	Yes
Skilled animators	Partially	Partially	No	Probably not[a]
Marketing team	No[b]	Yes	N/A	No
Actors	No	Yes	N/A	No
Stories	No[c]	Yes	N/A	No

[a]Only a handful of colleges offer the necessary training to work as an animator. Thus, one might believe that Disney could corner the market on the top animators, particularly if "the best want to be with the best." (This is an example of a scarce asset that may be more valuable at Disney than elsewhere.) However, other studios had excellent animators. *Ferngully* was a 1992 Fox animated feature that fared poorly at the box office but won awards for animation quality.
[b]There is no shortage of skilled marketing personnel. Other studios can outsource marketing or hire away Disney personnel, if necessary.
[c]Until *Lion King*, Disney's big animated hits were adaptations of well-known children's stories.

solid economic data. At the firm level, we recommend using a metric such as Economic Value Added. We are not able to measure EVA for the Walt Disney Studios, so we will use an alternative measure of performance: box office revenues. By examining box office revenues over an extended time period, we can assess whether brand name is the definitive Disney asset. Table 3.4 shows inflation-adjusted domestic box office revenues for Disney animated motion pictures released between 1986 and 1994. Disney's box office revenues increased fivefold to tenfold between 1986 and 1994. This is not the pattern we would have expected if Disney's key asset was its brand name. Disney's brand was very strong in the 1980s, helped by its long history and its extraordinarily successful theme parks.[6] Disney's brand might explain how *Oliver and Company* could pull in $114 million, but it cannot explain the remarkable success of Disney's "big four" movies: *The Little Mermaid*, *Beauty and the Beast*, *Aladdin*, and *The Lion King*.

Something must have happened in the late 1980s to early 1990s to elevate Disney's performance. Perhaps Michael Eisner, who took over the helm at Disney in 1984, had finally put his imprint on the Walt Disney Studios division. But Eisner was not actively involved in this division, and contributed little to the making of any of the hits of the early

Table 3.4
Domestic Box Office Revenues for Disney
Animated Motion Pictures 1986–1994

Title	Year Released	Domestic Box Office (2003 dollars)
The Great Mouse Detective	1986	$ 65 million
Oliver and Company	1988	$114 million
The Little Mermaid	1989	$166 million
The Rescuers Down Under	1990	$ 39 million
Beauty and the Beast	1991	$197 million
Aladdin	1992	$284 million
The Lion King	1994	$388 million

1990s. If credit is due to any one individual, it must go to another executive hired in 1984, Jeffrey Katzenberg.

Katzenberg was the chairman of The Walt Disney Studios division. He had responsibility for worldwide production, marketing, and distribution of all Disney's live action and animated motion pictures. By all accounts, Katzenberg was a hands-on executive, who increasingly came to micromanage all aspects of movie production, including the crucial tasks of fashioning the look and personality of the major characters (such as Scar and Simba in *The Lion King*). In 1994, Disney's second in command, Frank Wells, died in a tragic automobile accident. Denied a promotion to fill Wells's spot in the hierarchy, Katzenberg left Disney in 1995 to form Dreamworks SKG along with Steven Spielberg and David Geffin. (Katzenberg is the *K*.)

Let's examine a few more facts to see if they support the "Katzenberg was the key asset" theory. Table 3.5 augments the Disney box office history previously described. The data are completely consistent with the theory that Jeffrey Katzenberg represented Disney's most important asset. With the exception of *Tarzan*, no other Disney animated motion picture has come close to equaling the success of the "big four."

This is not to say that Katzenberg alone was responsible for Disney's success. After moving to Dreamworks, he had to replicate the resources and capabilities he had at Disney—hire animators, build up a marketing team, and so forth. Dreamworks' first animated release, *Prince of Egypt*, did a respectable $114 million in domestic box office, nearly matching Mulan's $137 million in the same year of release. In 2001, Katzenberg bested Disney. *Shrek* pulled in $278 million, more than three times the box office of Disney's *Atlantis*. Katzenberg was not infallible; Dreamworks' *Sinbad* was a box office disaster, grossing less than $35 million. But 2004's *Shrek 2* was another huge hit for Dreamworks.

Animated Assets?

Jeffrey Katzenberg is a mobile asset. For both personal and financial reasons, Disney failed to retain Katzenberg, who left in a pique. When he left Disney, Katzenberg took with him hundreds of millions of dollars of profits. The facts suggest that Jeffrey Katzenberg was

Table 3.5
Domestic Box Office Revenues for Disney
Animated Motion Pictures 1986–2001

Title	Year Released	Domestic Box Office (2003 dollars)
The Great Mouse Detective	1986	$ 65 million
Oliver and Company	1988	$114 million
The Little Mermaid	1989	$166 million
The Rescuers Down Under	1990	$ 39 million
Beauty and the Beast	1991	$197 million
Aladdin	1992	$284 million
The Lion King	1994	$388 million
Katzenberg departs	1994	
Pocahontas	1995	$171 million
The Hunchback of Notre Dame	1996	$117 million
Hercules	1997	$113 million
Mulan	1998	$137 million
Tarzan	1999	$189 million
102 Dalmations	2000	$ 72 million
The Emperor's New Groove	2000	$ 95 million
Atlantis	2001	$ 87 million

also a cospecialized asset. Since joining Dreamworks, he has replicated his Disney successes only on occasion. We may never again see a run of success such as he enjoyed with the "big four" movies. It seems that Disney and Katzenberg together accomplished more than the sum of Disney and Katzenberg apart. That is the essence of cospecialized assets.

Disney now faces the loss of yet another mobile asset. In 1991, Disney signed an agreement with tiny Pixar Studios to distribute their computer generated movies in exchange for a percentage of the box office. Following the success of 1995's *Toy Story* ($232 million domestic box office), Pixar and Disney signed an agreement to coproduce five additional movies. That agreement is set to expire soon. From Disney's point of view, Pixar is a partially mobile asset. Disney will certainly enjoy the profits from the next two movies released under the old contract. But then Pixar is free to negotiate with other studios. Pixar may wish to remain with Disney, particularly if there are joint assets (such as creative personnel from Disney and Pixar who work as a team). But Pixar's leverage gives it the upper hand. Even if Pixar stays with Disney, Pixar is sure to realize the lion's share of the profits.

WRAP-UP

We have now completed the theory of competitive advantage. To outperform their rivals, firms must create more B–C than they do. This requires scarce, immobile resources and capabilities. Even better, these should be scopable. Thoughtful completion of the R&C audit can provide a powerful *qualitative* assessment of the firm's B–C position. Ideally, this qualitative analysis should be backed up by facts about B and C. The next chapter presents a number of methods for generating these facts.

NOTES

1. An important question is "Why is Wal-Mart's distribution inimitable?" and we believe reading this chapter and Chapter 8 will enable the reader to answer this question.

2. This raises the related question of how firms develop expertise in innovation. This remains a challenge in the pharmaceutical industry, where firms with historically strong track records in R&D have had recent dry spells, while many new discoveries come from upstart companies.

3. This raises the issue of whether to buy the asset or enter into an arrangement such as an alliance where one firm uses the asset but does not take ownership. This issue cannot be resolved without substantial analysis of topics such as economies of scale, contracting, and incentives. The textbook *The Economics of Strategy* is a useful reference.

4. In theory, the athletes could unionize. Collectively, their talents are scarce, even if the talents of any one college athlete are relatively easily replaced. Thus, if they bargain collectively, they could command a large share of the revenues.

5. Of course, if their ideas paid off, these programmers got the benefit of profit *sharing* arrangements. These arrangements are an explicit way of assuring that the scarce talent does not extract all the profits.

6. Consider that while box office revenues grew by 500 percent, Disney's theme park revenue (inflation adjusted) increased by just 67 percent and much of that reflects expansion of Disney World.

CHAPTER 4

MEASURING YOUR COMPETITIVE ADVANTAGE: A TOOLKIT

Most managers believe that their firms outperform the competition. We call this logical impossibility the Lake Wobegon Syndrome, after the fictional town invented by humorist Garrison Keillor. In the town of Lake Wobegon, "all the women are strong, all the men are good-looking, and all the children are above average." Like children, alas, some firms must perform below average. An important challenge to every manager is to determine if their firm is among them.

Managers ought to have a healthy dose of confidence in their firms. But when it comes time for developing and assessing strategy, managers need to add a measure of reality. This often occurs when firms might consider weaknesses and threats during the course of a SWOT analysis. But such assessments rarely amount to anything more than brainstorming sessions.

If a firm is to accurately assess its strategic position, then it must explicitly measure its B–C. A quantitative assessment of B–C offers several benefits:

1. Measurement validates claims of superiority. There is no Lake Wobegon in the real world of business.
2. Quantitative measurement of B–C provides unmistakable evidence of a firm's long run economic viability. This is more reliable

than accounting data that can show short run profits at firms while masking the absence of long run prospects.

3. Quantitative data on B–C is necessary for optimal pricing and other tactical decisions.

Despite these advantages, strategic analyses rarely include rigorous quantitative assessments of B–C. This may be due to a lack of interest or a lack of the requisite analytic skills. These are not good excuses. Measurement is an essential element of strategy, and the required methods are well-known. The fields of business economics and marketing research offer a variety of approaches for quantifying costs and benefits. If a manager is not adequately tooled up to perform these calculations, rest assured that almost any good strategic management consultant can do them.

Before we describe these approaches for directly measuring B–C, we briefly discuss a closely related technique for keeping track of profitability: value added analysis.

VALUE ADDED ANALYSIS

Value added analysis is one of the best-known weapons in the strategist's arsenal. Developed by Michael Porter, value added analysis examines how profits accrue as production moves through the vertical chain from raw materials to manufacturing and, ultimately, retail sale. The term "value added" can be a bit misleading. From the perspective of strategic positioning, we define value as B–C—the difference between benefits and costs. Value added analysis examines profits—the logical consequence of value creation. Value added analysis is especially valuable when one is analyzing the performance of divisions and work units within firms, for which there may be no comparable performance measures. Mid-level managers may use value added to assess performance of a work unit in much the same way that senior executives and shareholders use corporate profits to assess the performance of a firm.

When all transactions take place among independent firms, value added and profits are one and the same. Value added is a much more useful tool when applied to divisions or work units within a vertically integrated firm. To perform a value added analysis for a division or work group, follow these steps:

1. Identify all the business units involved in the vertical chain.
2. Compute the profits that each business unit *would have enjoyed had it completed its transaction in an open market*, rather than inside the firm.

Step 2 requires the calculation of *transfer prices*. The correct transfer price of a good or service is the price it would have fetched in an open market, and a business unit's value added per unit produced is the difference between the transfer price of that unit and the cost of making it, which might, in turn, depend on the transfer prices of inputs used in production. Sometimes, it is easy for firms to determine transfer prices because there is an active external market for the good in question. At other times, finding a comparable external market transaction is difficult.

Here is an example of value added analysis when all the required prices are readily available.[1] Consider a firm, Gene Inc., which produces blue jeans. The firm sells its Gene Jeans to three different types of customers:

1. It sells unlabeled jeans to manufacturers that attach their own labels and sell the jeans as house brands.
2. It sells jeans under its Gene Jeans label (which it supports through extensive advertising and product promotion) to independent wholesalers, who then distribute them to retailers. (For simplicity, we suppose that the cost of affixing a label is zero.)
3. It sells some Gene Jeans directly to retailers, via self-distribution.

Gene Inc.'s value chain consists of three major activities: manufacturing, brand management, and self-distribution. Value added analysis determines the incremental profit each of these activities creates. Table 4.1 provides all the information necessary to compute value added.

Table 4.1
Volumes, Prices, and Costs for Gene Inc.

Total quantity of blue jeans manufactured	110,000 pairs per year
Unlabeled jeans sold to private labelers	20,000 pairs per year
Labeled jeans sold to wholesalers	80,000 pairs per year
Labeled jeans self-distributed	10,000 pairs per year
Selling price, unlabeled jeans	$4.00 per pair
Selling price, labeled jeans sold to wholesalers	$14.00 per pair
Selling price, labeled jeans self-distributed	$18.00 per pair
Production cost per unit, unlabeled jeans	$2.50 per pair
Total brand promotion and advertising expenses	$700,000 per year
Total cost of self-distribution	$20,000

We begin by computing total profits, which is the sum of the variable profits from each segment, minus aggregate promotion and distribution expenses:

$$\text{Total profits} = 20{,}000 \times (4 - 2.50) + 80{,}000 \times (14 - 2.50)$$
$$+ \ 10{,}000 \times (18 - 2.50) - 700{,}000 - 20{,}000$$
$$= \$385{,}000$$

We should bear in mind the bottom line figure of $385,000. When we add up the value added for each activity of the firm, we ought to get exactly this figure.

We proceed by assessing value added in each activity:

- *Value added in manufacturing* = profit that would have been made if all jeans were sold unlabeled to private labelers. We can compute the profit per pair to equal $4 − 2.50 = $1.50. At sales of 110,000 pairs of jeans, value added in manufacturing = $165,000.
- *Value added in brand management* = incremental profit made by selling 90,000 labeled jeans. To compute this, note that the transfer

price of manufactured jeans is $4, which is the price that Gene Jeans can get from the market for unlabeled jeans. The transfer price of selling labeled jeans is $14, the price of labeled jeans when sold to a distributor. Thus, the profit per pair of labeled Gene jeans (versus unlabeled jeans) is $14 − 4 = $10. The firm sells 90,000 labeled jeans, for a total profit of $900,000. Subtract $700,000 in marketing expense, for net value added in brand management = $200,000.

- *Value added in distribution* = incremental profit made by selling 10,000 labeled Gene Jeans via self-distribution. The profit for each pair of self-distributed jeans is $18 − 14 = $4. Ten thousand pairs generate profits of $40,000. Subtract $20,000 in distribution expense, for net value added in self-distribution of $20,000.

Note that the sum of the value added in each step ($165,000 + $200,000 + $20,000) is exactly equal to Gene Inc.'s total profits of $385,000.

Value added is useful for assessing strategy because it helps to identify the sources of profit creation within the firm. The most appropriate use of value added analysis is to examine changes in a work group's value added over time to see if performance has been improving or declining.

Value added analysis can be misused. Remember that value added requires value creation. Firms that focus on value added may not identify the underlying sources of competitive advantage. If you focus on competitive advantage, then value added should take care of itself. Another pitfall occurs when analysts equate the importance of a step in the vertical chain with its value added. Some analysts even assert that firms should cede low value added steps to the market. One should always compare such a recommendation to the next best alternative. Gene Inc. may create more value added from brand management than from any of the other activities it performs. This does not imply that it should perform brand management itself. That decision rests on whether Gene Inc. could be even more profitable if it outsourced brand management. Value added analysis cannot answer this question.

Ultimately, the success of Gene Jeans in the marketplace depends on whether the B–C created throughout the Gene Jeans vertical chain—

whether this involves Gene Inc. or independent firms—exceeds the B–C of competing brands. If Gene Inc. wants to know where it is positioned relative to rivals, it must measure benefits and costs. The tools for measurement that we describe next are an essential element of any introspective analysis of strategic positioning. Without applying these tools, firms can only guess as to their true strategic position.

QUANTIFYING COST ADVANTAGE

Most firms invest considerable energy in measuring their own costs. Modern accounting tools such as activity based costing (ABC) lend considerable precision to such calculations. It is much more difficult to assess rivals' costs. Yet doing so is essential for positioning analysis and also helps firms assess various tactics such as participating in price wars. Some firms are able to get good accounting data on their rivals; this is common in regulated markets. In the absence of accounting data, firms can use *activity cost analysis* to make reasonably educated guesses about a firm's cost position vis à vis the competition.

Many strategy texts describe activity cost analysis so we do not repeat the details here.[2] When possible, activity cost analysis applies precise cost accounting data to each step in the vertical chain of production for all competing firms. Such detailed competitive intelligence is rarely available. More often, the analyst must rely on economics, rather than accounting, to compare costs across firms.

The economic approach to cost comparisons begins by identifying the key *cost drivers* in production. Cost drivers include obvious factors such as local labor market conditions and taxes, as well as subtle factors such as worker productivity and costs of regulatory compliance. We identified many other cost drivers in the previous chapter, when we discussed opportunities for achieving cost advantage.

The next step is to weigh how each competitor stacks up on each cost driver. Who pays the highest wages? Whose workers are most productive? Whether by crunching some data or relying on third party research, it is sometimes possible to make fairly precise estimates of the resulting cost differentials. For example, consider the following cost drivers for hospitals:

- *Labor accounts for about half of all hospital costs.* A hospital in one community may face a soft labor market, allowing it to pay 10 percent lower wages than hospitals in other communities. This would give it a 5 percent cost advantage (just multiply the wage difference by the share of total costs: .10 × .50 = .05).
- *Inventory holding costs can amount to 5 percent of total costs at some hospitals.* A hospital that reduces its inventory holdings by a third, perhaps through just-in-time systems, can shave 1.66 percent off total costs (.05 × .333).
- *There are well-documented economies of scale in hospitals.* Research suggests that hospitals with 200 beds or more may enjoy 10 percent to 20 percent cost savings over their smaller competitors. There are also diseconomies of scale. Hospitals with 500 beds or more may be at a 5 percent cost disadvantage.

When it not possible to make precise estimates of cost differences, one must rely on more qualitative approaches. Though less rigorous, they may still point to important cost differences across firms. Here are the steps:

1. List the industry's cost drivers. Table 4.2 provides a generic list. The last row is labeled Others, acknowledging that specific cost drivers will vary by firm and industry.
2. Rate the cost drivers on a five-point scale according to their relative importance to total costs.[3] For example, if materials costs are a very small portion of total costs, then this should receive a rating of 1 (low importance). Fill in the column of data in Table 4.2 labeled Importance.
3. Rate each firm's relative position on each cost driver, again using a five-point scale. A rating of 1 indicates that the firm has a relatively low cost. Fill in the next column in Table 4.2.
4. Multiply the importance rating (column 1) by the relative position rating (column 2) and plug this Cost Driver Score into the last column.
5. The firm's overall position is the sum of its cost driver scores. The lower the score, the better.

Table 4.2
Cost Comparison Scorecard

Cost Driver	Importance (1 = high; 5 = low)	Firm's Relative Position (1 = most preferred position; 5 = least preferred position)	Cost Driver Score (Multiply columns 2 and 3)
Economies of scale			
Economies of scope			
Learning economies			
Capacity utilization			
Wages			
Labor efficiency (FTE per unit ` output)			
Materials purchasing costs			
Materials efficiency			
Others (specific to firm in question)			
			Overall Position =

Another way to evaluate a firm's cost position is to assume that the average competitor has a relative position of 3 on all cost drivers and compute the overall position of this average firm accordingly. Then rate your firm relative to the average and compute its overall position. Either way, you can obtain an often eye-opening evaluation of your relative cost position.

Table 4.3 shows a scorecard for Evanston Hospital in Evanston, Illinois. We placed considerable importance on labor costs as well as capacity utilization (due to the very large fixed costs and the presence of many empty beds in some hospitals). We have added an important cost driver that is specific to hospitals: patient severity. Economies of scale and scope that are not directly tied to capacity utilization, as well as learning

Table 4.3
Cost Comparison Scorecard—Evanston Hospital

Cost Driver	Importance (1 = high; 5 = low)	Firm's Relative Position (1 = most preferred position; 5 = least preferred position)	Cost Driver Score (Multiply columns 2 and 3)
Economies of scale	2	2	4
Economies of scope	1	1	1
Learning economies	2	1	2
Capacity utilization	3	2	6
Wages	5	5	25
Labor efficiency (FTE per unit output)	3	3	9
Materials purchasing costs	1	3	3
Materials efficiency	1	2	2
Severity of patients treated	3	5	15
			Overall Position = 67

economies, are of somewhat less importance to hospitals. Materials represent a relatively small portion of hospital costs and receive little weight in the analysis.

When scoring Evanston Hospital's relative position, we note that it is a large hospital operating near capacity. It has wide service offerings and considerable experience delivering complex medical procedures.[4] It also uses modern inventory management systems, helping to reduce inventory costs. Because it has a reputation for outstanding quality, Evanston Hospital tends to admit sicker patients than most of its competitors. This affects the severity score.

Evanston Hospital's overall position is 67. An average hospital that scored 3 on every cost driver would have an overall position of 63.

Evanston Hospital has a slightly higher cost position than its rivals, due largely to high labor costs and a relatively severe patient mix. Given its location in a wealthy suburb, it may be unable to do anything about the former. It may also be reluctant to turn away very severely ill patients, because they enhance Evanston's medical education program and allow the hospital to command a premium price. While striving to eliminate inefficiencies, Evanston Hospital's management accepts its cost position and has concentrated value creation activities on increasing B through new clinical programs that attract some of the region's top doctors.

In sum, ABC cost accounting is the best way to measure costs, but it is not helpful for measuring a cost position unless comparable data are available for a firm and its competitors. Absent such hard data, the firm should identify its cost drivers and complete a cost–comparison score-card. Such an exercise is valuable even when ABC data are available, be-cause it can help pinpoint the underlying source of a cost differential.

QUANTIFYING BENEFIT ADVANTAGE

Virtually every consumer goods manufacturer boasts about its quality. Some marketing efforts are legendary. Consider the lonely Maytag re-pairman who speaks of the appliance maker's reliability. But consumers do not have to take Maytag's word for it; independent ratings from *Consumer Reports* and others confirm Maytag's claims. In the same way, *Edmunds* reports that BMWs handle like a dream, and *Zagat's Restaurant Guide* rates Tru, Carlos, and Charlie Trotter's among the best restaurants in Chicago.

Thanks to magazines, web sites, and market research firms, it is fairly easy to obtain objective, qualitative rankings for many products and ser-vices, including airlines, electronics goods, sporting goods, movies, restaurants, hotels, automobiles, bicycles, books, music, and insurance companies. There are even report cards for hospitals and doctors. Most firms are savvy enough to pay careful attention to these rankings.

An accurate positioning analysis requires more than just qualitative rankings, however. Firms should try to measure benefits in dollars. Do-ing so pays off at two levels. At a tactical level, firms need to answer this question so they can set their prices optimally. At a strategic level, firms must be able to assign a dollar value to their B if they are to measure their B–C position. It is one thing for Maytag to know that its washers are reliable. It is another to know how much consumers value this reliability. Maytag cannot outperform its rivals unless the dollar value of reliability exceeds this cost. Only then can Maytag set a price high enough to cover its additional production costs without turning away customers. Put another way, Maytag cannot prosper from product reliability unless reliability brings with it a superior B–C.

When it comes to analytic methods, there are two types of benefits to consider. Some products yield dollar-for-dollar benefits; that is, the product reduces the amount that consumers must spend on other products. Fuel efficient hybrid cars are a good example. We measure dollar-for-dollar benefits by computing the *all-in cost* to consumers. Most products deliver less tangible benefits such as quality, convenience, reliability, and so forth. We can still measure the value of these benefits, in dollars, by borrowing methods from marketing research. These methods are so well established that they have been applied to seemingly metaphysical product benefits such as improvements to health and longevity. Before we discuss these marketing methods, we elaborate on measuring all-in costs.

Valuing Benefits by Measuring All-In Costs

Quantifying the all-in costs for different products is usually a simple exercise in algebra along the following lines: Suppose Honda invents a fuel efficient automobile engine that reduces a car's lifetime gasoline consumption by 2,000 gallons with no other effects on performance. If gasoline costs $2.00 per gallon, then the engine reduces all-in costs by $4,000. (For simplicity, we ignore the time value of money.) Consumers ought to be willing to pay up to $4,000 extra for Hondas equipped with this engine.

Here is a more complex example from an intermediate goods market, the market for cola sweetener. In this example, the choice of sweetener affects downstream production in a number of ways that are best captured through use of a *waterfall chart*. A waterfall chart resembles a stairway that climbs to a peak and then descends back down. The steps in the climb up measure the costs of key components of production using the existing technology. The steps back down measure costs using the alternative technology.

When purchasing sweetener for their flagship cola products, both Coke and Pepsi have two major alternatives: corn syrup and sugar. The price of sugar is about 3 euros per hundredweight of cola produced.[5] Corn syrup manufacturers want to know the price at which corn syrup is more attractive than sugar.[6] To determine this, it is necessary to compare the all-in costs of each alternative.

The waterfall chart in Figure 4.1 presents the comparison. The left-hand side (the climb up) shows the economics of cola production using sugar. In addition to the cost of the sweetener, the cola maker must pay for other materials, processing, and packaging. When the cost of sugar is 3 euros per hundredweight, all-in production costs are 17 euros per hundredweight of cola produced. (This is represented by the height of the middle bar in the figure.)

The right-hand side (the climb down) shows that by using corn syrup, the producer incurs somewhat higher processing costs and

Figure 4.1
Waterfall Chart for Cola Production

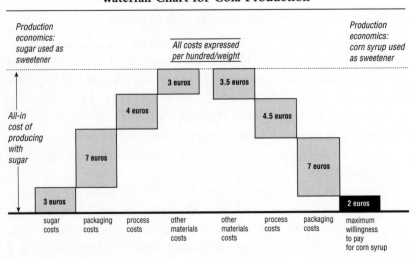

somewhat higher costs of other materials. Total production costs, not including corn syrup, are 15 euros per hundredweight of cola produced. This implies that Coke and Pepsi would be willing to pay up to 2 euros per hundredweight for corn syrup (the height of the last bar on the waterfall chart); at that price, the all-in cost for corn syrup and sugar are identical. In fact, the price of corn syrup is less than 2 euros per hundredweight. This is why every can of Coke and Pepsi lists corn syrup, and not sugar, as a leading ingredient.

Corn syrup makers could perform similar calculations for different segments of consumers (e.g., candy makers, producers of ready-to-eat cereal, and so on). This would identify all-in costs by market niche, allowing the industry to forecast product demand as a function of the relative prices of corn syrup and sugar.

Here is a quick summary of measuring tangible benefits:

1. Tangible benefits usually take the form of reductions in user costs.
2. Break out your user's production process into discrete steps.
3. Construct a waterfall chart. Going up, display the costs of each production step when customers use a rival product. Going down, display costs when customers use your product.
4. The final gap in the waterfall shows your benefit advantage or disadvantage.

Quantifying Intangible Benefits

In the previous example, we ignored the possibility that some consumers may prefer the taste of sugar over corn syrup. That was okay—few people can tell them apart. This is an unusual case; few goods are exactly alike in the eyes of consumers. Some are *vertically differentiated*; that is, there is a consensus on which is best and which is worst. Think Maytag for reliability or BMW for handling. Selling vertically differentiated goods is akin to pursuing a differentiation strategy; the firm generates more B for all consumers. This does not imply that the firm will control 100 percent of the market. Only some consumers are willing to pay the premium price that goes along with superior reliability or handling.

Other goods are *horizontally differentiated*; that is, some consumers prefer one product, while other consumers prefer another, even at the same price. There are many examples, including clothing, candy, movies, and family restaurants. Selling horizontally differentiated goods is akin to pursuing a niche strategy; the firm generates more B for some consumers and less B for others. Firms selling differentiated goods usually share the market, and each is able to charge a slight premium without driving away their loyal customers.

In many ways, differentiation and niche strategies are not that different. Differentiation may imply excellence in the eyes of all consumers, whereas a niche player has a small target audience that appreciates its position. But in both cases, firms create additional B–C for some consumers and set prices to optimally balance profit margins and market share. To assess their strategic positions, set optimal prices, and forecast market shares, both differentiated and niche firms must determine how much consumers value their product benefits *in dollars*. This requires that both types of firms answer the following question: How much are consumers *willing to pay* for the product? Measuring willingness to pay (WTP) is a staple of marketing research, but you do not require a marketing degree to understand how to do it.

MEASURING WILLINGNESS TO PAY

There are many highly valued products whose benefits can be summed up in a single word. Dove chocolates taste richer. Merrill shoes are more comfortable. Montblanc pens offer more status. These are examples where the product benefit can be captured more or less by a single dimension. In these cases, measuring B can be done in two steps:

1. Describe the benefit in qualitative terms.
2. Ask consumers how much they are willing to pay for this qualitative benefit.

The basic methodology for measuring WTP is quite simple. Researchers describe a product's intangible benefit to survey respondents.

They then ask the respondents how much they would be willing to pay for the benefit. A typical willingness to pay (WTP) survey might look something like this:

> Most washing machines cost $400 and break down two times in seven years. How much would you be willing to pay for a washer that cleans just as well, but only breaks down one time in seven years?

The answer provides a direct measure of the WTP of reliability, and Maytag or any other manufacturer can use the answer to set prices. In a similar way, one can measure the B of improving almost any attribute of almost any product.

WTP Example: Putting a Dollar Value on Health

Researchers have used WTP methods to put a dollar value on good health. The U.S. Environmental Protection Agency (EPA) has cited the results to justify the high costs to firms that must comply with EPA regulations such as installing scrubbers in the smokestacks of coal burning plants. In other words, the EPA has shown that when it comes to scrubber regulation, the B more than offsets the C.

The EPA began with environmental studies showing the extent to which scrubbers can clean up the air, and with epidemiological studies showing that cleaner air and water lead to reduced incidence of medical conditions like headaches and nausea. These are obviously very important benefits to our health, but are they worth the high cost of regulation? To translate the benefits into dollars, the EPA commissioned the renowned National Opinion Research Center (NORC) to measure consumer WTP for improved health.

NORC asked thousands of individuals to respond to questions along the following lines:

> Consider sinus problems that cause congestion and pain in your sinuses and forehead all day. You may even need to blow your nose every few minutes. How much would you be willing to spend to avoid a day of sinus problems?[7]

Based on the responses to such surveys, the EPA estimated that eliminating sinus problems is worth about $50 per day and eliminating nausea is worth about $75 daily. When multiplied by the incidence rates, these dollar benefits exceeded the cost of adding smokestack scrubbers, and justified the regulations.

Some researchers have asked about the value of life itself, using survey questions like this one:

> Suppose that your current life expectancy is age 80. A new health program would offer a 10 percent chance of extending your life expectancy to 82. How much would you be willing to pay to participate in such a program?

Multiplying the response by 5 and correcting for discounting (the benefit is not enjoyed until many years from now) results in the value of a year of life today.[8] Based on responses to questions like this, researchers peg the value of a year of life to the average person at about $100,000.[9] Drug companies use these results to demonstrate the value of their new discoveries as well as to defend price increases.

Improving WTP Survey Methods

A few respondents to the NORC/EPA survey gave implausibly large answers—as much as $5,000 to avoid a day of sinus problems. This is not uncommon; open-ended WTP surveys often generate excessively large estimates. There are a variety of approaches to more accurately gauge WTP.[10]

One approach is to compute the median response, rather than the mean. This minimizes the effect of outliers, but ignores all other useful valuation information. (For example, it would be impossible to draw a demand curve on the basis of the median alone.)

Here is an attractive alternative:

1. Pick some starting point for valuation of the benefit. Call this $X.
2. Ask the respondents if they would be willing to pay more than $X for the benefit.

3. If the answer to 2 is yes, increase the amount until you find the point where they say no. This tipping point is their point of indifference—their WTP. (Do the opposite if the answer to 2 is no. Again, the tipping point is their WTP.)

This simple approach avoids outliers. But beware, because the initial choice of X tends to bias the response. If you start with a larger X, you will get larger valuations.

The next approach requires many more survey respondents but is immune from these biases. We use specific numbers to illustrate how this approach works.

1. Pick a range of plausible valuations for your product benefit. In this case, we use benefits ranging from $0 to $100. Divide these into round number increments, that is, $0, $10, $20, . . . , $100.

2. Count the number of increments and divide the number of respondents by this number. If there are 11 increments and 220 respondents in your sample, you should assign 20 respondents per increment. Don't worry if you are inexact.

3. Start with the first increment, $0. Ask if the first the respondent would pay more than $0 for this benefit. Record the answer. Repeat for all 20 respondents assigned to this increment. Record the fraction of respondents who said yes.

4. Repeat for each remaining increment. When you have finished, you should be able to complete something like Table 4.4. (This table is based on a survey of Kellogg students concerning their willingness to pay each month for more accessible parking on the Northwestern University campus.)

We can immediately derive a demand curve from these responses. With a bit of algebra, we can also compute the WTP for the average student. Note that this method requires that the increments are identical, in this example, $10. It is also essential that we begin at

Table 4.4
Responses to WTP Survey

Dollar Amount	Percent Saying Yes
$ 0	.95
10	.90
20	.75
30	.60
40	.50
50	.40
60	.25
70	.20
80	.10
90	.05

$0. Here are the necessary steps. Don't worry; it is really rather simple.

1. Let ρ_x represent the fraction of respondents who said they would purchase the benefit at price X (e.g., when X = $30, ρ_x = .60).
2. Add up all the ρ_x for all values of X in the survey. Call the sum P_x. In this example, P_x = 4.70.
3. Let η represent the amount of the increment in X (e.g., η = $10).
4. Multiply $\eta \times P_x$. This represents the WTP of the average survey respondent. For our Kellogg students, WTP = $47.

Now that you know the WTP for your product benefit, you can evaluate your strategic position and price your product accordingly. In this case, Northwestern administration knows that good parking is highly valued by Kellogg students, and it can even estimate the additional revenue that would be generated were it to take the controversial step of raising prices for the most convenient spots.

WTP for Diversely Differentiated Products

Many products are *diversely differentiated*, that is, they vary along many dimensions. *Consumer Reports* rates washing machines on reliability, but it also reviews how well they clean, their energy efficiency, and convenience. Automobiles have even more points of differentiation, from dry pavement braking time to rear legroom. Diverse differentiation complicates strategic positioning analysis by increasing exponentially the variety of comparisons across products. Even so, the process really boils down to two basic steps. First, identify the most salient dimensions of differentiation. Second, compute the WTP for these dimensions. The most straightforward way to do this—perform a WTP survey on each dimension—is also the most time consuming. Fortunately, researchers may select from several other tools for valuing diversely differentiated products. These tools, *conjoint analysis*, *hedonic pricing* analysis, and *multinomial choice* modeling, are all based on the WTP concept.

Conjoint analysis relies on carefully constructed surveys to measure WTP for each attribute without having to ask about them one at a time. Firms can use conjoint analysis to identify differences in WTP by customer segment. Hedonic pricing relies on actual transactions to determine WTP. Hedonic pricing does not normally account for customer segmentation. Multinomial choice modeling incorporates the best of both techniques, relying on actual transactions while accounting for segmentation. It is also the most difficult to implement.

All three approaches treat products as if they were bundles of attributes. For example, we can think of a family sedan as a bundle of product features, including Interior Space (I), Acceleration (A), Fuel Economy (F), and the number of Safety Features (S). Consumers have a WTP for each dimension that we can label WTP_I, WTP_A, WTP_F, and WTP_S. All three approaches use the same algebraic equation to express the WTP for a family sedan with a specific combination of features:

$$WTP = (WTP_I \times I) + (WTP_A \times A) + (WTP_F \times F) + (WTP_S \times S)$$

Where the approaches differ is how they compute the individual feature WTPs.

We describe briefly how each approach works, so as to point out the potential value that these marketing research tools hold for strategic analysis. It may be best to leave their application to the professionals.

Conjoint Analysis

In conjoint analysis, researchers ask survey respondents to express their preferences for specific bundles of attributes. The researchers choose a variety of bundles whose dimensions have been manipulated to maximize the power of the survey. Using regression analysis, the researchers can determine how each consumer values each dimension. Continuing the automobile example, researchers might ask a series of questions along the following lines:

The next time you purchase a car, how likely is it that you would select a car with the following attributes? Please circle a number from 1 to 10 to indicate your feelings.

- Seats 5 adults
- Accelerates from 0–60 in 9.0 seconds
- Gets 25 miles to the gallon
- Has 2 airbags
- Price = $22,000

Would definitely   Definitely
not purchase   would purchase

1   2   3   4   5   6   7   8   9   10

The researcher asks each respondent to give their preferences for about 20 different cars, each with different combinations of features and price. Regression analysis reveals the values of WTP_I, WTP_A, WTP_F, and WTP_S.

Hedonic Pricing

Like conjoint analysis, hedonic pricing computes the value of each product attribute. The key difference is that hedonic pricing analysis uses data on actual purchases, whereas conjoint analysis relies on surveys. The advantage of hedonic pricing is that consumers do not always behave as they claim they will in surveys; there is no substitute for data on actual purchases. The disadvantages are that hedonic pricing models cannot be applied to new product attributes (e.g., valuing airbags prior to their introduction) and, for statistical reasons, require many product offerings relative to the number of product dimensions.

The basic idea behind hedonic pricing is very simple. The researcher obtains data on product prices and attributes. Regression analysis reveals the dollar value of each attribute. There are many simple applications of hedonic pricing methods. For example, waiting times are an important attribute of many goods and services, such as gasoline. Gas stations that have higher prices tend to have shorter lines. Regressing gasoline prices on waiting times and other product dimensions (location of the gas station, brand name, etc.), it is possible to infer the negative value that motorists place on waiting (lending precise meaning to the expression "time is money"). Published studies show that the amount a typical consumer is willing to pay to save time waiting in line for gas is highly correlated with the hourly wage they receive at work. This provides an important rule of thumb about time-saving convenience benefits:

> The dollar value of the benefit of time-saving goods and services roughly equals the time saved multiplied by the consumer's hourly wage.

There are many other applications of hedonic methods. The housing industry uses these methods to determine how much space to devote to bedrooms, kitchens, and lavish bathrooms. Hedonic methods show computer makers the market value of faster processors and bigger hard drives. Hedonics show pharmaceutical companies the value of reducing side effects. Hedonics can even provide estimates of the value of a life.

Hedonic pricing studies that measure the value of a life treat risky jobs as a bundle of attributes, including wages and risk to life and limb. Using highly detailed data about these and other job characteristics, economists have estimated the market trade-off between risk and wages, all else equal. From these estimates, economists infer the value of a life. The most credible estimates put the value of a life at about $6 million. Other hedonic studies of wages and job risks put the value of a year of life at about $200,000, or about twice the value obtained from surveys. Studies like these can provide powerful information for firms seeking to set the right price, as the next example shows.

The Hedonic Value of Life and Genentech's tPA

Sophisticated health care purchasers, including U.S. insurance companies and government agencies overseas, are often faced with a health/dollar trade-off. They can purchase lifesaving state-of-the-art medical technologies, but only at a very high price. A rule of thumb that has been embraced by many purchasers is that new technologies are worth the price, provided the price does not exceed about $60,000 per year of life. (Note that this is less than the value of life obtained from surveys and hedonic methods.) This rule of thumb proved to be crucial to biotech company Genentech when it stood ready for a critical product launch in 1987. A fledgling company at that time, Genentech was banking heavily on the success of a break-through cardiovascular drug, tissue plasminogen activator, or tPA. An anticlotting agent, tPA is prescribed for patients suspected of having had a heart attack. Prior to the introduction of tPA, the agent of choice was streptokinase, priced at $200 per dose. Although it was not much more costly to produce, Genentech set the price of tPA at $2,200 per dose, and hoped that health care purchasers would pay a premium price for a premium product.

At first, there was little medical evidence to suggest that tPA was better than streptokinase. Many purchasers balked at the significant price difference. Skeptical government agencies in Europe and Canada were especially reluctant to foot the bill. Five years after its launch, tPA was foundering. But in 1993, researchers published results from a large scale international clinical trial comparing outcomes for patients randomly assigned to either streptokinase or tPA. The results were great news for Genentech. The mortality rate for patients who had received tPA was 6 percent. The mortality rate for patients who had received streptokinase was 7 percent. The difference of 1 percent was statistically significant.

Genentech could prove that tPA offered a higher B than streptokinase. It still had to convince payers that the value of the higher B more than offset the higher C. This was a matter of algebra. An extra $2,000 bought an additional one percentage point chance of survival. This meant that the expected cost of saving one life was $200,000. Genentech computed the dollar value of the benefits as follows. At that time, a heart attack survivor could expect to live an average of six additional years. Using a value of a year of life of $60,000, this put the benefit of the life saved at $360,000, or nearly twice the cost. Most purchasers found this benefit/cost argument compelling and agreed to cover tPA.

Multinomial Choice Modeling

Some of the most important recent advances in measuring WTP are the direct result of three related phenomena:

1. Availability of highly detailed consumer-level data sets, such as supermarket scanner data.
2. Reductions in costs of computing.
3. Advances in statistical research methods known as multinomial choice models.

Multinomial choice models are used to analyze situations where consumers select from several choices. The researcher uses transaction-level data about actual consumer choices, prices, product attributes, and consumer characteristics. Supermarket scanner data are ideal for this purpose, especially when the consumer uses a store discount card (such as the Safeway Select card used by shoppers at the Safeway and Dominick's grocery stores) that permits the researcher to match consumer identifying information to actual purchases. Recent advances in statistics even allow researchers to substitute regional market shares and regional demographic information for transaction level data.

Multinomial choice methods are highly technical; we know of no MBA program that teaches them. However, more and more doctoral programs in economics and marketing teach these methods. Without going into details about how to implement these methods, we do want to list some of the questions that these methods can answer with great precision:

- How much is the typical consumer willing to pay for a product with a specific combination of features?
- How will WTP change if the firm changes one product feature?
- What types of consumers most highly value certain features?
- What is the predicted market share for a product with a given combinations of features and price?
- What is the overall benefit position of each seller in the market?
- For which customer niches does the seller provide the greatest benefit?

Here is an example of how we used these methods to help a managed care organization (MCO). MCOs assemble networks of health care providers. Their enrollees must choose a provider from the network. Because patients are very sensitive about the availability of providers, it is important for MCOs to offer attractive networks.

In the past, MCOs have relied on hospital market share information to evaluate their networks. MCOs figured that hospitals with high shares must be very popular with consumers. But market shares can be misleading. A hospital with a high share may actually have close substitutes for many nonessential services such as minor surgery. At the same time, a hospital with a low share may offer unique services to a small but important subset of the population, such as those requiring advanced cardiovascular care. Given a choice of access to just one of these hospitals, patients may prefer the latter. Using multinomial choice models, we obtained highly detailed information about the demands of all types of patients for all available hospitals in a metropolitan area, and computed the value that each hospital added to the network. Insurers have used this information to help create networks that maximize consumer value at a minimal cost.

WRAP-UP: WHY WE MEASURE

We have seen SWOT analyses that are all conjecture and no facts. We have also seen positioning analyses performed by world famous consulting firms and costing sizable six figure sums that are equally long on qualitative claims and equally short on analytics. This usually leads to a Lake Wobegone Syndrome, where all firms believe they are above average. If a firm believes it is positioned to outperform its rivals, or is in the unfortunate position of lagging its rivals, it should be able to find tangible evidence of this by examining its B–C. If it cannot find hard evidence of its B–C position, then maybe it should reassess its beliefs.

In this chapter, we have described many tools from the fields of economics, accounting, and marketing that can be used to measure B and C. Some managers will be comfortable using these tools themselves; others will leave the analyses to professionals. Given the stakes involved in being right about your B–C position, there is little excuse for failing to obtain the facts.

NOTES

1. You may want to refer to a graduate level accounting text for details about how to compute transfer prices.

2. Thomson and Strickland's *Strategic Management* (Homewood, IL: Irwin Publishers, 2002) provides a nice example for the beer industry.

3. Any point system will do, of course.

4. For details on how to estimate the exact slope of a learning curve, see Besanko et al. (2003).

5. A hundredweight is a unit of weight. The numbers used in this example are for illustrative purposes only and are thus not based on the actual production costs of any particular soft drinks producer.

6. From a taste and calorie standpoint, we assume the choice of sweetener is immaterial.

7. In reality, the surveyors spend considerable time describing the symptoms, so that respondents get a good feel for associated benefits of good health.

8. A 10 percent chance of living two extra years means an expected life extension of 0.20 years. Thus, the value of one year of life is five times the value of this expected life extension.

9. Does $100,000 seem low, particularly when you consider the multimillion-dollar lawsuits that abound in the United States? Remember how the above question is framed: "How much would you pay to live one more year starting now?" This is a different question from: "How much does the party who takes one year of life away from you owe you?" Economists refer to this as the "endowment effect" and it is a bit of a puzzle. Individuals value what they have (or are endowed with) in excess of what they would be willing to pay to acquire the same thing.

10. See A. Boardman et al., *Cost-Benefit Analysis*, Upper Saddle River: Prentice Hall, 2001, for more details on these approaches.

CHAPTER 5

THE CANCER OF COMPETITION: HOW TO DIAGNOSE IT

In any market, the firms that create the most B–C are usually the ones with the highest profits. But just how profitable will they be? And are firms that fail to maximize B–C doomed to years of lackluster financial performance? Positioning analysis is not sufficient to answer these questions. The profits of any firm depend on the overall profitability of the industry in which it competes. A relatively profitable firm in the airline industry, such as Southwest, has lower risk adjusted returns on investment than average firms in many other industries, while average tobacco firms, such as Brown and Williamson, enjoy relatively high risk adjusted returns.

The profits of a firm depend as much on the performance of its industry as they do on the performance of the firm relative to its industry. The following equation says it all:

$$\text{Profits of Firm X} = \text{Profits of Firm X relative to average firm} \\ + \text{Profits of average firm}$$

Positioning tells us about relative profits, but not about the profits of the average firm. To learn the latter, we must perform an industry analysis, such as the Five Forces Framework described in Chapter 1. The centerpiece of any industry analysis is competition—the jockeying for position among firms in a market. Competition can eliminate the gap between prices and costs that is essential for profits. Even in a market in which all firms generate high B–C, competition can drive prices down toward costs, so that all the value is captured by consumers (P is close to C). If competition is absent, P–C may be high, and even average firms may do handsomely.

Competition (or internal rivalry, in Five Forces lingo) can afflict an industry like a cancer. Left undetected, competition may intensify and spread, threatening the survival of all but the hardiest competitors (those creating the most B–C). Early detection of competition can help firms avoid its worst consequences. An important role of the strategic analyst is to diagnose the competitive conditions of the marketplace and anticipate when they are likely to turn virulent. In this chapter, we describe a set of symptoms that indicate when competition is likely to destroy profits. While no single symptom is definitive in the diagnosis, each additional symptom increases the likelihood of harm. As symptoms pile up, managers must either prescribe a course of action to reverse them, or give up the hope of profitability. We examine potential cures in the next chapter.

When it comes to diagnosing competition, many managers are hypochondriacs. In our experience, managers performing either a Five Forces analysis or the *OT* component of SWOT are quick to complain about competitive pressures. It is true that most firms face some degree of competition, but not all forms of competition destroy profits. Competition is sometimes benign (what economists call "soft competition"), and competing firms are able to capture most of the value they create. Firms need to properly diagnose the nature of rivalry they are facing and fashion an appropriate response. It is a mistake to respond in the same way to all types of competition; poorly judged responses can trigger the kind of fierce competition firms should be trying to avoid.

Analyses of competition should not be limited to output markets. Firms also compete in input markets: hiring workers, purchasing raw materials, and so forth. As with output markets, competition in input markets takes value that might have accrued to firms and transfers it to others: workers, suppliers, owners of target firms. Input market competition can be just as harmful as competition in output markets. Tom Hicks, the owner of the Texas Rangers baseball club, learned this lesson the hard way. Hicks thought he was competing with other owners for the services of all-star shortstop Alex Rodriquez when he offered a record shattering $200 million contract. It turned out that Rodriquez had no comparable offers and the Rangers operated in the red until they traded Rodriquez and his contract to the New York Yankees.

Whether examining input or output markets, firms should be most concerned about the kind of malignant rivalry that destroys profitability without stimulating industry demand. Firms in this situation face intense competition, dwindling profit margins, and an uncertain future. The first step to avoiding or curing this malignancy is to perform diagnostic tests: to accurately determine the intensity and likely consequences of the competition the firm is facing.

HOW COMPETITIVE IS MY MARKET?

We have asked hundreds of Kellogg executive education students—most of whom have product line profit and loss responsibilities—"How would you characterize competition in your market?" Whether the owner of a health club, a senior executive at an auto parts manufacturer, the founder of an Internet startup, or a nursing home administrator, our exec ed students invariably give the same, short answer. They tell us that competition is "intense." If they do not say it is "intense," they say it is "fierce." Even a student who worked at the local power monopoly, Commonwealth Edison, insisted that competition was intense.[1] Not one student has ever described competition as "soft" or "benign."

From what we can gather, virtually all managers believe they face intense competition because they are trying vigorously to succeed and are constantly looking over their shoulders at firms that might threaten their success. But the concept of "intense competition" loses its meaning when it is used to describe dramatically different competitive conditions. Surely, the competition faced by Commonwealth Edison, the only supplier of residential electric power in Illinois, is not the same as that faced by another Illinois firm, ATF Inc., which is one of dozens of firms that supplies screws and other metal parts to the automotive industry.

The diagnosis for competition is not equally dire in all markets. Some markets, such as airlines, appliances, and metal screws, have minuscule profit margins that leave even the best performers on the brink of bankruptcy. In many other markets, such as prescription drugs, semiconductors, and residential power, even average firms enjoy long-term profitability. If a doctor issued the same foreboding diagnosis of terminal cancer to every patient, regardless of the symptoms, malpractice suits would quickly pile up. Doctors offer dire diagnoses with caution. The same proviso must apply to diagnosing competition. *Managers should not confuse a concern about competition with its effects on the bottom line.* If the concept of "intense competition" is to make any sense, it cannot apply equally to all competitive situations.

Steps Toward Making a Diagnosis

It takes four years of medical school and even more time in residency training before a physician can confidently diagnose cancer and prescribe a treatment. Fortunately, markets are not as complex as the human body. A large body of economics research has been devoted to identifying consistent symptoms of competition, and there are many heuristics that facilitate a reasonably accurate diagnosis. A proper diagnosis requires paying attention to the following:

- The "Who" of competition: Identify the competitors. Many of the symptoms of competition depend critically on the number of competitors, their objectives, capabilities, and financial condition.
- The "How" of competition: Identify the competitive levers. Competition is harmful because it drives prices down toward costs. The extent of damage depends on whether firms compete to win customers directly on the basis of price, or whether other product attributes such as quality are more important.
- The "Symptoms" of competition. Knowing "Who" and "How" sets the stage for a step-by-step evaluation of each of the symptoms of competition.

The remainder of this chapter discusses the Who, How, and Symptoms of competition. But first we offer one caveat.

The Substitute Conundrum

We do not spend much time in this book discussing substitutes—another of Porter's Five Forces. The reason to worry about substitutes is simple enough: They nibble away at demand. But an analysis of internal rivalry should consider whether substitutes might affect competition. We offer some specific examples in this chapter, but first offer some general principles.

Just as firms face competition from rivals within their industry, an industry faces competition from other industries. Competition within an industry often reduces vulnerability to these substitutes by improving the industry's B–P profile. In this way, seemingly destructive competition loses some of its edge. At the same time, firms that compete in several markets simultaneously, such as multinational firms competing globally, may find that competition in one market forces them to toughen up in ways that benefit them in other markets. Hence, domestic rivalry may lead to higher global demand as an industry is advantaged on the product and/or production side relative to the same industry in other nations.[2] The pharmaceutical industry, dominated by U.S. drug makers who face a variety of novel competitive challenges in the U.S. market, is a good example.

This is not to say that industries should welcome competition from substitutes. Usually, the destructive effects of competition in the home market outweigh any benefits in fighting off substitutes or competing in foreign markets. Even so, firms should pay attention to these peripheral effects, as they may shape how they react to perceived competitive pressures.

WHO: IDENTIFYING THE COMPETITORS

The first symptom of destructive competition is the presence of many competitors. Often, this fact alone is enough to draw reasonable conclusions about the intensity of competition. The Com Ed/ATF comparison is just one example of an empirical regularity:

All else equal, markets with more competitors are more competitive.

Knowing something about each competitor's history, cost structure, and motivations permits a further refinement of the diagnosis. This makes competitor identification a good starting point for the analysis of competition.

Most managers can readily name their main competitors. A BMW dealer will list Mercedes Benz, Lexus, Acura, Cadillac, Infiniti, and Audi, but not Hyundai, Saturn, Subaru, or Chevrolet. It is easy to identify what distinguishes these two lists. Cars on the first list feature high performance and at least a touch of luxury. Cars on the second list do not.

This gut feel approach to competitor identification is not bad, but it does have its limitations. BMW has a broad product line, ranging from sports sedans to SUVs. The list of competitors differs by product line. Potential buyers of the BMW X5 sports utility vehicle would certainly consider the Mercedes 320ML and the Acura MDX. But they might also consider the Lincoln Navigator or even the Porsche Cayenne. It is not clear whether potential buyers of the BMW 325 would consider a Porsche Boxter, and there is no way that the Lincoln Town Car would make their shopping list.

This example demonstrates the value of identifying competition at the level of the product, not at the level of the firm. It is also important to identify competition in each input market. If firms face different competitors in each segment of their market, then the diagnosis of competition might also vary by segment. Also bear in mind that many firms sell in more than one geographic market and may face different competitive conditions in each. It is vital to get this sorted out.

Table 5.1 offers a step-by-step process for competitor identification for the output markets served by a particular firm or industry. (A parallel process applies to competitor identification in input markets.) A key part of this process is the ability of the analyst to define competition differently in each unique product and geographic market. This is critical to industries such as airlines, which serve thousands of origin/destination pairs, and pharmaceuticals, which treat hundreds of diseases in scores of nations. Firms in these industries may face very different competitive conditions in each product/geographic market they serve.

There are a variety of ways to complement this qualitative assessment with rigorous data analysis. Industrial competitors in the

Table 5.1
Competitor Identification

Step 1	*Initial market selection:* Define the product markets of interest—presumably a list of the markets in which the firm competes. This is essentially a list of broad product markets. Each of these markets will be narrowed by following steps 2 to 5.
Step 2	*One product market or several?* Assess whether the competitors are likely to be the same for all the products you have selected. If you are not sure, then do not assume they are. If you believe the set of competitors is likely to be the same, then choose one product to study. Otherwise, be sure to repeat steps 3 to 5 for each product.
Step 3	*One geographic market or several?* Identify the different geographic regions in which the product is sold. If you believe the set of competitors is likely to be the same in each region, then pick one region to study. Otherwise, repeat steps 4 to 5 for each region. (Note: If competition varies by product and by region, the number of distinct markets to study can rapidly proliferate. This is not an excuse for pretending that competition is the same in each product/region, however.)
Step 4	Identify the key *product performance characteristics.* What does the product do for consumers? Here you should specify the features that drive customer choice: • Do customers prefer a "one stop shop" or do they prefer to deal with multiple vendors? • How might the product be segmented by attributes like look and feel, ease of use, warranties, durability, availability of complementary goods as well as other relevant factors consumers are likely to consider in choosing among industry offerings? • What types of service contracts are firms offering? • What different channels is the product distributed through? • Does brand matter and why? • How intimate are relationships between firms and customers? What are the switching costs? • How much price dispersion is there in the market? What drives this price dispersion?
Step 5	*Competitor identification:* Identify the set of firms whose products deliver comparable specifications on the key product performance characteristics. These firms constitute the market.

United States, Canada, and Mexico will usually *belong to the same industry code* using the North American Industrial Classification System (NAICS).[3] Competitors' products should be subject to the same forces of supply and demand, so that *prices of competitors should show a high degree of correlation over time.* Consumers view competitors' *products as alternatives*: If one firm unilaterally lowers its prices, its competitors should lose market share.[4] Whenever possible, one or more of these empirical analyses should be used to validate competitor identification.[5]

Market Structure

Recall that markets tend to be more competitive when they have more competitors. Once competitors are identified, it is trivial to count them. The number of competitors is a measure of *market structure*, an important piece of evidence when diagnosing competition. But a simple count of the number of competitors can miss important details, by failing to distinguish between a market like microprocessors, with a dominant firm (Intel) and many smaller players, and a market like dishwashers with several equal size competitors. A computationally simple alternative is the *four-firm concentration ratio*, which is the market share controlled by the four largest firms.[6] Though useful and widely cited, the four-firm concentration ratio also fails to distinguish between a market controlled by one large firm versus one controlled by three or four midsize competitors.

A better measure is the *Herfindahl index*. The Herfindahl captures fine distinctions in market structure based on the market shares of the largest firms. Here is how to compute the Herfindahl:

1. Obtain data on each competitor's market share. You can ignore firms with shares below 2 percent.
2. Square the shares. For example, if one firm has a share of 0.40, its squared share is 0.16.
3. Add the squares. For example, if one firm has a share of 60 percent and its rival has 40 percent, the Herfindahl equals $.6^2 + .4^2 = 0.52$.

Note that the Herfindahl equals 1 if there is a lone monopolist and is close to 0 if many firms divide the market and no firm has a market share above 10 percent.

In general, competition becomes more benign as the Herfindahl increases. (In contrast, competition becomes more virulent as the four-firm concentration ratio increases.) Borrowing from (and slightly modifying) U.S. Department of Justice guidelines on competition and antitrust, we offer an explicit statement of the first symptom of destructive competition:

> *Symptom 1:* The Herfindahl index is below .25 and/or has recently decreased in magnitude by at least .05.

Market structure is not the only determinant of competition. If no other symptoms of competition are present, a market with a Herfindahl of .25 or less can be quite profitable. The U.S. tobacco industry provides a case in point. Long divided among six major firms, the Herfindahl has hovered between .20 and .30 for nearly a full century. Yet few other symptoms of competition have emerged in this industry, and all the major tobacco firms have enjoyed enviable returns on assets. Only the recent decline in demand associated with highly publicized health risks and local regulations on public smoking have managed to dampen industry earnings.

Measuring the Herfindahl is only the first step in diagnosing competition, and a low or declining Herfindahl is just one symptom. Before presenting a full list of symptoms, it is necessary to examine more deeply the ways in which firms attempt to gain market share.

HOW FIRMS COMPETE: THE COMPETITIVE LEVERS

A quick look at three industries—soft drinks, pharmaceuticals, and hospitals—reveals the rich variety of competitive levers that firms may pull in their efforts to outperform their rivals.

Coke and Pepsi have been in competition for more than a century and have dominated the cola market for nearly all that time. Coke has the larger market share, though new product introductions and high profile advertising campaigns have yielded market share movements of one or two percentage points annually. This does not sound like a big swing in share, but small gains in a multibillion-dollar market are a cause for celebration. The Cola Wars, as this competition is often dubbed, sometimes resemble the battle between the Germans and French along the western front during World War I, with great effort but little movement to show for it. It is no wonder that Coke and Pepsi executives routinely characterize their rivalry as fierce.

For the past half century, about 20 major pharmaceutical firms have dominated the research, development, and marketing of prescription drugs. Throughout this time, drug houses such as Merck, Abbott, and Pfizer have sought out dominant positions in key drug categories like antibiotics and cardiovascular care. To win market share, they engage in patent races, hoping that massive R&D investments will generate defensible patents on new drugs. The stakes are high: Successful drugs generate billions of dollars in annual profits. Pharmaceutical executives routinely describe their competition as intense.

U.S. hospitals compete to fill beds. To do that, they must attract doctors. A hospital that lands a top heart surgeon or orthopedic specialist can expect to dominate that line of business in its local market. Prior to the growth of managed care and the resulting emphasis on cost containment, hospitals competed for doctors by offering them generous staff support and the latest in medical technology. From the doctors' point of view, these expenses improved the quality of their work environment. Hospital administrators described the competition to land doctors as vigorous.

As these examples show, firms may pull any number of levers in their efforts to win market share. Although firms in the industries just described rely on different competitive levers, the industries have two important features in common. First, they have been very profitable for a long time. Advertising soft drinks, developing drugs, and providing state-of-the-art medical technology are all costly endeavors, but as long as these industries can keep prices well in excess of costs, there are plenty of profits to go around. In fact, the prices of colas, prescription drugs, and hospital services are all at least double the variable costs of production. This compares favorably to typical manufacturing firms, where prices usually exceed variable costs by roughly 50 percent.

The high price–cost margins are the result of another feature shared by these industries: an historic absence of price competition. The result is that firms can increase spending on advertising, R&D, or medical technology and then pass the costs along to consumers by raising prices. Competition on these nonprice dimensions may seem fierce, but it often leaves ample profits for the competitors. When we think of competition that destroys profits, we should think of *price competition* and its most lethal manifestation, price wars. Airlines immediately come to mind as an industry that has been ravaged by price wars. But many other industries are susceptible. Newspapers, airframe manufacturing, breakfast cereals, online brokerage, microprocessor chips, and diapers have all experienced bouts of deep price reductions and heavy financial losses.

Some Price Wars

English billionaire Rupert Murdoch, CEO of News Corporation, is no stranger to price wars. His newspapers in Australia and the United Kingdom (U.K.) have been engaged in numerous battles over the past two decades. In 2002, News Corporation's U.K. *Sun* tabloid newspaper engaged in a bitter round of price cutting with the *Daily Mirror*. With prices dropping to 20p nationwide, and as low as 10p in some places, the *Sun* lost more than £7 million per month.

In the mid-1990s, U.S. cereal makers such as Kellogg's and General Foods enjoyed 100 percent markups above variable costs. This attracted entry by off-brand cereal makers, triggering a lengthy price war that drove down retail prices by 20 percent or more. The effect on the bottom line has been staggering; the stock price of Kellogg's (the only pure play cereal maker) has been essentially flat since 1994, while the S&P 500 has increased nearly 200 percent over the same period of time.

An unusual and highly publicized input market price war erupted four decades ago when the fledgling American Football League (AFL) took on the established National Football League (NFL) in the market for star players. It began in 1965, when New York Jets owner Sonny

Werblin signed University of Alabama quarterback Joe Namath to a deal paying an unprecedented $427,000 for the first year. When the AFL's Denver Broncos made a big offer to University of Illinois star Dick Butkus, the NFL assured the future Hall-of-Famer that he would receive "wheelbarrows" full of money if he signed with them. (He chose the NFL's Chicago Bears.) Soon, both leagues were giving wheelbarrows of money to players like Roman Gabriel, John Brodie, and Pete Gogolak. After Oakland Raiders head coach Al Davis became the AFL's commissioner in April 1966, the bidding wars intensified. The AFL, which had never been profitable, took big losses, and the NFL lost money for the first time in more than a decade. Both leagues quickly came to their senses, and by June 1966, they agreed to merge. Soon thereafter, Al Davis returned to the front office of the Oakland Raiders, where he has enjoyed a legendary career building teams within the rules of the monopoly NFL.

In all of these examples, firms relied on prices to build market share (whether in output markets or input markets), and their industries suffered grievous harm. This gives us one of the most telling symptoms of destructive competition:

> *Symptom 2:* Firms rely on price reductions to gain market share. (Input market corollary: Firms rely on wage increases to obtain best inputs.)

By the time this symptom appears, it is often too late to save the industry from heavy losses, as the preceding examples show. Fortunately, many symptoms appear long before competition devolves into price wars. Before we identify them, we should discuss a bit further the effects of nonprice competition on profits.

Nonprice Competition

As discussed, nonprice competition is *usually* benign, because firms that push nonprice levers as they jockey for market share can usually raise prices to cover their costs. There is one big caveat: The price increases must not drive consumers toward substitute products. This could happen if the nonprice enhancements are of marginal value and the industry demand is very elastic (that is, the industry price elasticity of de-mand is much bigger than 1).[7] In this case, industry price increases can result in substantial revenue reductions as consumers drift toward substi-tute products or do without. Thus the third symptom of destructive competition:

Symptom 3: Nonprice competition combined with a large industry price elasticity of demand.

Looking back at our three industry examples of nonprice competi-tion, we would expect the demand for prescription drugs and hospitals to be very inelastic, because these are highly valued products and ser-vices with few good substitutes. In fact, good research pegs these indus-try elasticities at around 0.10 to 0.30, which is low compared to most other industries. As long as other symptoms of competition are not se-vere, pharmaceutical companies and hospitals can compete on nonprice dimensions, pass cost increases along in the form of higher prices, and maintain their profitability.

On the other hand, we would expect the industry elasticity of de-mand for colas to be rather large. (One estimate pegged the elasticity during the 1980s at about 1.1.[8] The recent proliferation of noncola beverages has made Coke and Pepsi drinkers more price sensitive, dri-ving the elasticity higher.) Facing a high industry elasticity, Coke and Pepsi cannot easily pass along their costs of advertising. They have felt the sting; nonprice competition like the Cola Wars ad campaigns is tak-ing a gulp out of industry profits.

PRICE COMPETITION

A firm that wants to increase its market share can pull nonprice levers, but this can take time, drive away customers (through any accompany-ing price increases), and may not even be feasible (if product enhance-ments are difficult to deliver). Price reductions are often the only surefire way to gain market share.

Price reductions invariably boost sales, at least until rivals have a chance to respond. Sales increases, in turn, drive revenue growth, provided the firm's own price elasticity of demand is greater than 1.[9] Firms risk many dangers when they pull the price lever, however. One problem is that revenue growth is at least partially offset by cost increases associated with increases in production and sales. A bigger problem is that any increase in sales almost always comes at the expense of rivals, who are likely to respond by lowering their own prices. In the end, all firms may end up with about the same market shares that they started with, with possibly higher volumes (depending on the industry elasticity of demand), but at much lower prices and profit margins. A widespread industry price reduction is almost never good for industry profits.[10]

These price reductions have a kind of multiplier effect on profits; a 1 percent reduction in price usually causes much more than a 1 percent reduction in profits. To see why, consider a typical U.S. manufacturing firm, where production costs represent about 70 percent of total revenues. (In other words, the gross profit margin is 30 percent.) For this firm, a 5 percent price reduction would reduce the gross margin to 26.3 percent, effectively chopping 12.3 percent off the share value of the firm. Table 5.2 provides an idea of the multiplier effect for seemingly innocent 5 percent price reductions and more substantial 20 percent reductions.[11] With such large multiplier effects, deep and prolonged price wars can cripple an industry. Just ask Kellogg's and the other breakfast cereal makers, or any of Rupert Murdoch's newspaper rivals.

Table 5.2
The Price War Multiplier

Gross Margin in Peacetime	Price Reduction	Gross Profit Margin during Price War	Percent Decline in Gross Profit Margin
20%	5%	15.8%	−21.0%
30%	5%	26.3%	−12.3%
40%	5%	36.8%	−7.9%
20%	20%	0	−100 %
30%	20%	12.5%	−58.3%
40%	20%	25.0%	−37.5%

TRIGGERING PRICE COMPETITION

Rupert Murdoch was not ignorant of the risks associated with launching a price war. Most managers understand the risks, but many cut prices anyway. When they weigh the short- and long-run benefits and costs, they find that market conditions make price cutting a worthwhile gamble. The conditions that favor heavy price cutting constitute the remaining symptoms of a market that is ripe for harmful competition.

To help identify the symptoms, bear in mind that managers will not usually cut prices unless three conditions are satisfied:

1. They have exhausted nonprice competitive levers.
2. They believe that the price reduction will generate sufficient increases in sales so as to be worth the risk of retaliation.
3. They are unconcerned about the subsequent effect on industry profits.

Condition 1 is often satisfied; many managers find that nonprice levers are too costly and time-consuming, and have no guarantee of success. They turn to price reductions, which are fast and usually quite effective. Condition 2 is required because no manager could justify a price hike that did not boost sales, even if rivals did not retaliate. Condition 3 follows from the fact that price reductions by one firm almost always translate into lower profits for the industry. A firm that reduces its own price must care only about its own profits, and dismiss the effects on its industry.

A variety of factors associated with demand, sales transactions, and competition all contribute to the temptation to reduce prices. A thorough analysis of these factors reveals the remaining symptoms of harmful price competition.

The Nature of Demand

Few firms reduce prices just to be nice to their customers. They reduce prices to increase sales and market share. This will likely provoke rivals to match prices in response. Rivals might even slash prices further, provoking a price war. Even so, a firm that reduces its prices can generate profits in both the short run (prior to rivals responding) and the long (after rivals respond). Here is why:

- In the short run, the firm will enjoy the benefits of undercutting its rivals. It will steal the business of price sensitive customers.
- In the long run, after rivals have responded and the dust has settled, some of the customers who switched to the price cutting firm may not switch back. The firm may end up with a higher market share than initially. This increase in share may hold, even if industry prices creep back up.[12]

These effects suggest two related symptoms that can lead to intense price cutting:

Symptom 4: Customers are price sensitive.

Many factors influence customer price sensitivity. Product differentiation, personalized service, and favorable locations all contribute to consumer loyalty and reduce price sensitivity. Switching costs, which make it difficult for consumers to try new products, also reduce price sensitivity. The next chapter describes how firms use these tactics to insulate themselves from price competition.

Symptom 5: Customers are willing to switch loyalties, even if they try a new product just once or twice.

Price reductions encourage price sensitive customers to break from old shopping patterns. A few will be pleasantly surprised by the new products, and when prices equilibrate, they will not switch back. Loyalty switching usually goes hand in hand with price sensitivity. Consumers who are willing to try something new just to save a few dollars must not have been wedded to their old product in the first place. Thus, a key condition that makes price cutting profitable in the short run (lack of loyalty) might make it profitable in the long run as well. This assumes that the price cutting firm can cultivate its newly won customers.

New firms entering established markets are often eager to reduce prices to encourage customer switching. When the new entrant has deep pockets and can sustain a prolonged spell of low prices, it can cause a substantial disruption in the status quo. In 2003, Washington National Bank invaded the Chicago consumer banking market by offering no-fee checking accounts and free ATM services. Several area banks responded by reducing their own user fees. National's aggressive pricing is not unusual for large firms entering new markets. Nestlé, the world leader in infant formula, slashed prices when it entered the U.S. market in the late 1980s. Microsoft aggressively prices new software products in categories it has yet to dominate.

Symptom 6: A large firm has entered into an established market.

Competition can take an ugly turn when consumers have few loyalties. Firms will aggressively reduce prices, hoping that a money losing customer today will translate into a cash cow tomorrow. For decades, General Motors (GM) used this strategy by luring first time car buyers with cheap, low margin Chevrolets and Pontiacs, and then watching them move up to Buicks and Oldsmobiles, and, eventually, high margin Cadillacs. Thanks in part to this strategy, all car makers struggled to make a profit at the low end of the market. Nowadays, a young GM car buyer is apt to move up to a Toyota and then to a BMW and GM is no longer willing to sell Chevrolets at a loss; as a result, the entire entry-level category is more profitable. The strategy of selling low at market outset, and selling high when the market matures, remains a cornerstone of many emerging technology markets, such as cellular phone and Internet service.

Once a market takes off, the imperative to slash prices disappears. Firms find they cannot produce enough to meet current demands, let alone steal business from rivals.

Thus, we have our first counter symptom:

Counter symptom 1: Industry demand is growing rapidly, and firms are producing at capacity.

Conversely, firms with excess capacity may find that they are better off selling product at prices below average costs than not selling at all; they can at least make a small contribution toward fixed costs. Hence:

Symptom 7: The industry has excess capacity.

This symptom is especially worrisome if marginal costs are well below average costs, so that price reductions leave the industry in an unsustainable position. Industries with high fixed costs relative to variable costs are therefore especially susceptible to the ravages of price wars, and this symptom must be watched closely. Again, the airline industry offers a perfect example. American Airlines' recent campaign to increase legroom by removing seats was viewed by many observers as a tactic to increase customer B, but American surely understood that the tactic was easily copied and could not create a competitive advantage. Though never stated publicly, it is more likely that American hoped its strategy *would* be copied, as this would reduce industry capacity and limit the risk of price wars. Unfortunately for American, its competitors were reluctant to risk losing market share and did not follow suit.

The Nature of the Transaction

A price cutting firm hopes to reap quick, large benefits. How quickly, and how large, will depend on how long it takes for its rivals to respond, and how much business it can transact in the interim. This suggests the next symptom:

Symptom 8: Prices are kept secret from the competition.

It seems counterintuitive, but secret pricing encourages price cutting. To understand why, consider a company bidding on a supply contract, where the low bid will win. Suppose it has one rival who also covets the contract. If the firm lowers its bid and its rival learns about the price cut, it will match immediately. This defeats the purpose of the price reduction, and eliminates price cutting as an effective strategy. Rather than compete on price, the firm may choose to compete on other dimensions that are not easily matched. With the emphasis off price competition, the winning bidder is likely to enjoy higher prices and higher profits.

Now suppose the bidding is secret. The firm can undercut its rival without prompting an immediate reaction. This gives the firm reason to cut its price. One problem, the rival is thinking along the same lines. Not only that, each firm likely knows what its rival is thinking and there is nothing they can do about it. Suspicions like these fuel further price reductions, and a not-so-secret price war gets underway.

This dynamic occurs all the time in virtually every market in which purchasers put contracts out for bid. Think of Northwestern University purchasing health insurance on behalf of its approximately 7,000 faculty and staff. It wants an established insurer, so it seeks bids from United Healthcare of Illinois, Blue Cross of Illinois, CIGNA, and Humana. All four firms offer comparable health insurance products. All have similar costs and can afford to offer family coverage for about $6,000 per year. Let's think about how competition is likely to play itself out.

Suppose that United Healthcare of Illinois offers to sell insurance at a price of $7,000. The other three insurers learn about this offer and know they could profitably undercut it, but would they? If a competing insurer offered insurance at a price of $6,800 and this offer was made public, United would immediately match it. Thus, United's competitors would have no reason to offer a lower price. If they are smart, all three rivals would match United's bid of $7,000 and compete on other dimensions, such as customer service.

These insurers compete for the business of many other organizations. If the Northwestern contract prices are made public, rivals may even learn to trust each other not to slash prices with other customers. As long as each firm toes the line at $7,000, they will continue to fight it out on nonprice dimensions. Secret pricing, on the other hand, breeds distrust. The losing insurer would suspect that it was substantially underbid (as opposed to losing on nonprice grounds) and will price more aggressively the next time around. This will provoke aggressive responses, launching a cycle of price wars.

Northwestern's 7,000 employees represent a modest percentage of a health insurer's business. Imagine how much greater is United

Healthcare's temptation to cut prices if it is bidding on the insurance contract for Abbott Laboratories' 70,000 employees. Thus the next symptom:

Symptom 9: Transactions are lumpy and large relative to annual sales.

Many businesses contract to sell their goods and services in large quantities that represent a substantial share of annual sales. In a typical year, Boeing and Airbus are lucky to receive orders from just a handful of commercial air carriers. Heavy duty truck engine manufacturers may sign just a few production contracts in a year. Many houseware makers rely on Wal-Mart and Target for 10 percent or more of their annual sales. Firms that bid on lumpy contracts have extra incentives to bid aggressively.

Think about health insurance again. When United bids for Abbott's business it certainly understands that an aggressive bid might cause the competition to bid aggressively on this and other contracts. But it might not care. Aggressive bidding on the Abbott contract offers the promise of large revenues, a large market share, and maybe even large profits. Aggressive bidding might trigger retaliatory price cuts, but even if that occurs, it will be for future deals and probably with smaller clients. A large bird in the hand is worth several small birds in the bush, and Abbott is one of the largest birds in the nation. United might not give the same consideration to smaller clients, out of fear of triggering a price war. But it might put such fears aside for Abbott's business.[13]

Large buyers like Abbott often feel entitled to deeper discounts. Their size alone can often provoke sellers to price aggressively, but this is not etched in stone. Sometimes, smaller buyers may demonstrate greater price sensitivity, and this can promote heated price competition even when larger buyers find it hard to get discounts. A good example is the substantial discounts that mail order pharmacies negotiate with the makers of brand name prescription drugs. Unlike their larger chain drug store rivals, mail order pharmacies stock a limited selection of drugs and are very selective in choosing the drugs they make available.

Misreads and Misjudgments

Firms may understand the risks of price cutting and privately voice that if their rivals toe the line, they will, too. (Public utterances of that sort would be blatant violations of antitrust law.) But how should they respond in the event that a rival crosses the line and reduces prices? The knee-jerk reaction would be to match the reduction. This is usually the correct reaction; failure to match prices will encourage even further aggressive pricing. But sometimes the knee-jerk reaction is the wrong reaction. The climax to the 1983 movie *WarGames* offers a telling example of the importance of patience.

In the movie, Matthew Broderick plays David Lightman, a teenager who hacks into a North American Aerospace Defense Command (NORAD) computer to play what he thinks is a harmless simulation called Global Thermonuclear War. Lightman takes the Soviet side and launches a surprise first strike on the United States. The NORAD computer does not know it is a game and plans a massive counterattack, one that would trigger a real global thermonuclear war. Thanks to some clever detective work (Lightman figures out the NORAD computer's password), the world survives intact. In the end, the NORAD computer announces that "The only winning move is not to play."

Close competitors often feel like opposing military forces facing off against each other. Neither wants to fire the first shot, but neither will sit back and take punishment if the other attacks first. Problems will arise if, as in the movie, a firm makes a real response to an imagined act of aggression by a competitor. If competitors are to avoid their own version of *WarGames*, they must carefully monitor each other's actions lest they accidentally trigger an unwanted price war.

One danger is that competitors might *misread* each other's decisions. That is, they think their competitor has reduced price and intends to steal market share, but it has not. (In *WarGames*, the computer misread David Lightman's actions, incorrectly believing that missiles had been launched.) Table 5.3 gives another example offered by two McKinsey Consulting strategists who examine the pricing of automobile tires. Tire makers sell their tires to dealers such as Sears and NTB at an invoice price that is observable to the competition. But tire makers also make

Table 5.3
Potential for Misreads

	Goodyear	Michelin	Observed or Secret?
Invoice	$35	$32	Observed
Volume Bonus	$ 3	$ 0	Secret
Marketing Allowance	$ 2	$ 0	Secret
Net Price to Dealer	$30	$32	Secret

hidden concessions to dealers, such as volume bonuses and marketing allowances.

When Goodyear observes Michelin's $32 price, it may assume (incorrectly) that Michelin is also extending volume bonuses and marketing allowances, and may infer that Michelin has lowballed the price. The reality, though, is that Goodyear has the bargain price. The secretive nature of pricing may cause Goodyear to trigger a retaliatory price war, slashing its prices even lower. At some point, Michelin would have to respond, and industry profits would quickly dissipate. Apparent price reductions are not always what they seem. The pricing of many products is very complex, making it difficult to determine if a rival has actually reduced prices.

It is also important to understand the motive for a price reduction. A firm might slash prices on a sluggish product line, fully intending to maintain high prices on its other products. Its rivals might *misjudge* the price cut to be the start of an aggressive ploy to boost market share. If they respond with broader price cuts, a price war could ensue.

These examples of misreads and misjudgments give us Symptom 10:

Symptom 10: Firms set prices in a complex environment, where it is difficult to monitor each other's actions and intentions.

The Competitors

Price reductions and price wars are not possible unless individual managers with pricing responsibility choose to slash prices. The motives of managers can matter as much as the market environment. There are two symptoms to look for when searching for managerial-driven price wars.

Symptom 11: Managers have strong motivation to increase market share.

Maximizing profits and maximizing market share are often diametrically opposed; the fastest way to boost market share is usually to slash profit margins. Despite numerous such admonitions from business economists, many firms are driven by market share objectives, rather than profitability. The results can be disastrous.

Many companies learned this lesson at the end of the tech bubble. Consider Lucent Technologies, which, under former CEO Richard McGinn, was consumed by market share objectives. McGinn informed division managers that if they failed to meet their share targets they would miss out on millions of dollars in bonuses and risk termination. Lucent's managers protested that product innovation and marketing efforts had their limits, and that market share growth would require setting prices below costs. McGinn held fast to the market share goals, and losses mounted while investors questioned accounting practices (such as early booking of sales so as to boost current period revenues). In little more than a year, between March 2000 and April 2001, Lucent lost 93 percent of its share value.

Lucent is not the only company to reward managers for share growth. Sometimes, the complexities of accounting, especially within a large diversified firm, make it too difficult to measure the profits attributable to any one product. It must seem better to give a tangible goal, such as market share growth, than no goal at all. We think this is a mistake and regard Lucent as the poster child for "market share at all cost" thinking. Unfortunately, some firms have little choice but to reward market share growth, because their rivals are doing the same. After all, high prices are well and good, but only if you are selling product.

Even if managers have their eyes on profits, circumstances may force them to take a short-term view. This also encourages price cutting:

Symptom 12: Firms are overly focused on the short term.

Most business owners are in it for the long haul and would not sacrifice the future for a quick buck.[14] Their managers do not always take the same long view. Some managers receive bonuses based on meeting current period objectives. (This raises the question of why owners would give managers such short-sighted rewards.) Other managers may plan to leave the firm before long (and may want to buff up the resume with a record of solid sales growth). Whatever the reason, when managers focus on the short term, price cutting often results, usually at the expense of the firm's owners.

Sometimes, firms and owners are equally focused on the short run. This is especially likely when firms are struggling to survive, such as startups and established firms on the brink of bankruptcy. Time and again, the U.S. airline industry provides compelling examples of this dynamic. During the past 20 years, nearly every major U.S. carrier has been in or near bankruptcy. Unable to pay off debts, these airlines need quick infusions of cash. They understand that price reductions are unlikely to boost market share substantially; computerized yield management systems guarantee that rivals will immediately match prices. They are still tempted to cut prices, however, to take advantage of the many passengers who are willing to "time shift" their purchases by buying tickets today for flights they intend to take in the future. This provides a much needed short-term infusion of cash, though often at the expense of future profits. This may explain why industry leaders like American Airlines' former CEO Robert Crandall fought hard to limit government subsidies of struggling carriers. In his view, it was better for the industry to let them exit quickly than to let them linger on in price-cutting desperation.

Some carriers, such as Southwest, slash prices because they have dramatically lower costs than their rivals. Price cuts enable Southwest to grow steadily and prosper at the same time. This is a good example of a very common symptom of pricing instability:

Symptom 13: There are substantial differences in production costs across firms.

The resulting price cutting is not bad for all firms, but will devastate those with high costs.

FACILITATING PRACTICES

Many managers lament that they would enjoy higher prices if only their rivals would learn to trust each other enough to share in the benefits of pricing stability. Occasionally, firms engage in *facilitating practices* that make such trust possible, even inevitable. Facilitating practices can offset many of the symptoms that trigger intense price competition:

> *Counter symptom 2:* The firms engage in facilitating practices.

Perhaps the most common facilitating practice is *price leadership*. One firm, usually the industry market share leader, announces an annual price hike. The rest of the industry follows suit shortly thereafter. For decades, Kellogg's was the breakfast cereal industry price leader. Annual price increases, matched by General Foods, Post, and the rest, assured healthy profits. Unfortunately for these industry giants, Kellogg's pushed prices so high that off-brand cereals were able to overcome steep entry barriers and win a substantial share of the market. This led to the industry price war previously described.

There are many other facilitating practices, some tailor-made to specific industries, many on the borderline of antitrust laws. We discuss some of the classic examples in the next chapter.

WRAPPING UP: MAKING THE DIAGNOSIS

Table 5.4 presents a checklist that can assist in the diagnosis of destructive competition. When working through the checklist, remember that no one symptom is definitive, but several in combination could be a telltale warning of dangers ahead. Be sure to assess the current status of the symptoms, as well as whether they are getting worse over time. Sudden changes in the wrong direction could indicate the likelihood of lethal competition in the future, even if current conditions seem benign.

Table 5.4   Diagnostic Checklist

Symptom	Current Status	Trend
Herfindahl index.		
Firms rely on price reductions to increase share.		
Nonprice competition in the face of a large industry price elasticity of demand.		
Price sensitive customers.		
Customers are willing to switch loyalties to new products.		
A large firm has entered into an established market.		
The industry has excess capacity; marginal costs are well below average costs.		
Secret pricing.		
Large, lumpy transactions.		
Complex pricing with potential for misreads/misjudgments.		
Managers with pricing authority have market share objectives.		
Managers focus on short-term results.		
Substantial differences in production costs across firms.		
Counter Symptom	**Current Status**	**Trend**
Market demand is growing.		
Firms have facilitating practices.		

NOTES

1. Com Ed was concerned that some consumers might switch from electric appliances to gas powered appliances. Most companies would be delighted to be limited to such minor competitive concerns. The tendency of monopolists to overstate competitive pressures is not unusual. In its federal antitrust case, Microsoft characterized competition as "vigorous." The federal judge was not persuaded, and found that Microsoft possessed monopoly power in the operating system market.

2. M. Porter, *Competitive Advantage of Nations*, New York: Free Press, 1990.

3. These codes, which replace the Standard Industrial Classification (SIC) system, may be found at the NAICS web site, www.census.gov/epcd/www/naics.html. Codes for service firms are under development.

4. Economists have developed even more sophisticated tools for market identification that are especially useful for establishing monopoly power in antitrust cases. These usually require both data and statistical methods that are beyond the grasp of the typical analyst. The interested reader with a strong economics background might start with T. Bresnahan, "Empirical Studies of Industries with Market Power," in R. Schmalensee and R. Willig, eds., *Handbook of Industrial Organization*, Amsterdam: North-Holland, 1989.

5. Antitrust enforcers say that a group of firms constitute a well-defined market if, in the event that all of those firms could legally collude on price, they would implement a nontrivial (e.g., 10%) increase in price. This would indicate that there were no other firms constraining their pricing; hence the firms in question represented the entire market of interest. Unfortunately, testing this hypothetical involves sophisticated statistical analysis of data that is often hard to come by.

6. In a similar way, one can compute a 2-firm ratio, 8-firm, and so forth.

7. The industry price elasticity of demand is the percentage change in industry sales for each 1 percent change in industry price. This contrasts with the firm level price elasticity of demand, which equals the percentage change in a firm's sales when it unilaterally changes price by 1 percent. The latter is usually much larger in magnitude, because the price-hiking firm's customers may switch to other firms in the industry, rather than cease buying the product altogether.

8. F. Gasini, J. J. Lafont, and Q. Vuong, "Econometric Analysis of Collusive Behavior in a Soft-Drink Market," *Journal of Economics and Management Strategy* (Summer 1992): 277–311.

9. It had better be bigger than 1. Basic economics states that if the own price elasticity is smaller than 1, the firm will surely boost profits by *raising* its price.

10. An exception might be if the industry price elasticity of demand has increased substantially, so that current prices are much too high. This seems to be what happened

to compact disks, where Internet piracy by young adults sharply increased the price sensitivity of this dominant consumer segment.

11. If industry demand increases as a result of the price reduction, then the overall effect on profits will be somewhat smaller than the amount reported in the table.

12. Chapter 7 considers a third possibility: The price reduction will drive rivals from the market.

13. One way for health insurers to avoid aggressive pricing is to centralize pricing decisions at the national level. Individual contracts will seem less lumpy, and the consequences of retaliation will be more apparent. But no insurer would want to move first. If United centralized, but CIGNA and Aetna did not, United might be more thoughtful about avoiding price wars, but it would lose a lot of business in the process.

14. Owners do discount the future of course, and we do not mean to suggest that a dollar tomorrow is worth as much as a dollar today. But few owners would give up two dollars tomorrow for one today.

CHAPTER 6

THE CANCER OF COMPETITION: HOW TO CURE IT

$\mathbf{T}$hink of B–C as a pie to be divided among competitors and consumers. Were it not for competition, this value might be divided as shown by the top pie in Figure 6.1. Consumers would get some share of the value, but the lion's share would go to the competitors. Most firms are not so fortunate; competition eliminates the P–C gap, resulting in a division of value that is more accurately depicted by the bottom pie.

If managers want to partake from the pie at the top instead of the one at the bottom, they should keep the following ideas in mind:

- *An ounce of prevention is worth a pound of cure.* Create conditions for your firm and industry to minimize the intensity of price competition.
- *Be thy brother's keeper.* Your actions may harm competitors; their responses may do the same to you.
- *People who live in glass houses should not throw stones.* Some markets are more prone to price wars than others. If you cannot eliminate the conditions that precipitate price competition, then try to avoid throwing the first stone.
- *He who laughs last laughs best.* In the worst case scenario, price wars devolve into wars of attrition. If such a battle looms, it is essential to determine if and how you can win it.

Figure 6.1
Competition and the Division of Value

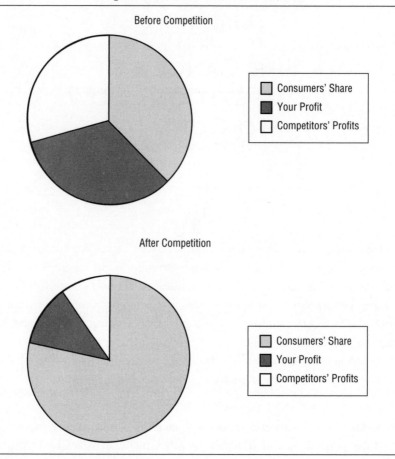

Before Competition

Consumers' Share
Your Profit
Competitors' Profits

After Competition

Consumers' Share
Your Profit
Competitors' Profits

Of course, it never hurts to increase the size of the pie. We touch on this idea later. For a further discussion of the variety of partnership strategies that can increase overall industry B–C, we direct you to Adam Brandenberger and Barry Nalebuff's *Coopetition*.[1]

AN OUNCE OF PREVENTION

Like many cancers, price wars are often preventable. Firms can prevent price wars either by taking unilateral actions that soften pricing pressures, or through coordinated actions that facilitate peaceful coexistence among competitors. We describe both strategies.

Unilateral Actions—The Importance of Targeting

Of all the symptoms of potentially dangerous price competition, perhaps the two most important are the number of competitors and high consumer price sensitivity. There is often little that a firm can do to limit the number of competitors (though we discuss entry deterrence in the next chapter). But firms may be able to reduce consumer price sensitivity and, in the process, soften price competition.

There are two ways for a firm to reduce the price sensitivity of its customers:

1. Find ways to uniquely meet customer needs.
2. Make it difficult or costly for its customers to find acceptable alternatives.

In either event, the firm can increase its price without losing substantial market share. By the same token, if competitors lower their prices, the firm need not feel compelled to respond. The result is softer price competition, because price is no longer an effective competitive weapon.

To uniquely meet consumer needs, the firm must select the correct target market. Most managers fully understand this cardinal rule: *Do not target a market that has been targeted by others!* It is almost impossible to overstate the benefits of finding a market niche that can insulate the firm from competition. In fact, if you scratch the surface of firms that have reputations for being ferocious competitors, you will often find a history of competitor avoidance.

Consider two exemplars of competitive strategy, Wal-Mart and Southwest Airlines. For all of the discussion about the former's efficient distribution systems and the latter's efficient operations, it is easy to overlook the fact that, until recently, both firms thrived by avoiding competition. Wal-Mart grew by opening stores in small towns whose populations were large enough to support one mass merchandiser, but not two. Exploiting simple scale economies and its developing distribution expertise, Wal-Mart trounced the local mom-and-pop competition without having to go head to head against Sears, and other big mass merchandisers. Through its local "mini-monopolies," Wal-Mart enjoyed unrivaled profitability. Wal-Mart's continued growth allowed it to match Sears and Penney's on sheer size, and to use its fully developed distribution expertise to displace its older rivals in the urban markets that it had wisely shunned in its early history.

Southwest Airlines has a similar story. Southwest began in 1973, making short commuter flights from its home base at Dallas' Love Field to underserved cities such as Corpus Christi and Lubbock. As it grew, Southwest remained a puddle jumper, flying largely on short routes between mid-sized cities. It enjoyed monopoly status on routes like New Orleans to San Antonio while avoiding hotly contested routes like New York City to San Francisco. This strategy was partly due to Southwest's fleet; it flew only Boeing 737's with limited range. But this was also clever targeting. Many of Southwest's routes were busy enough to support one point-to-point carrier, but not busy enough for two.

Southwest pursues the same targeting strategy today. It continues to be the only major carrier on many of its routes. When it does enter more competitive markets, it targets secondary airports, especially those near downtown. Not only does this keep costs down, it allows Southwest to lure customers with strong preferences for the smaller, often conveniently located, airports.

Southwest and Wal-Mart differentiated themselves through careful targeting of geographic markets. Other firms have avoided competition by targeting along other dimensions. Enterprise entered the car rental market to serve customer segments deemed unworthy by the renters operating at airports. Enterprise was especially successful opening rental outlets near auto body shops. Thanks to this novel strategy, nearly 40 percent of car renters today do so in their home market. Like Wal-Mart and Southwest, Enterprise discovered that targeting a specific (and underserved) customer does not mean limited opportunities for growth, and can generate healthy profit margins.

Sometimes, firms seem to face many competitors in their target market, yet still remain immune to price competition. The key to their success is loyal customers who would rather pay a premium price than try another seller. One might call this the Krazy Glue Approach to softening price competition, because it relies on customers who are stuck on their established buying relationships.

Unilateral Actions—The Krazy Glue Approach

Although Krazy Glue is one of the most recognized brand names, few customers know that the key ingredient, ethyl cyanoacrylate, is used in many competing products. Even so, Krazy Glue dominates the market, charging as much as twice the competition without driving away its customers. Firms can insulate themselves from pricing pressures by following Krazy Glue's formula for success: Find ways to make customers stick to you.

Many companies succeed by developing a loyal customer base. These consumers are willing to pay a premium price because they believe they are receiving premium quality. All successful brands depend on such consumer beliefs, even if they sometimes leave competitors scratching their heads in disbelief. Sometimes, brand loyalty is associated with product image. Most of our Kellogg colleagues are hard-pressed to taste the difference between Coke and Pepsi on the one hand, and RC Cola or Safeway Select on the other. Yet we would never be caught dead hosting a party for our colleagues at which we served the latter (lest our friends think we were destitute!). We will leave it to the psychologists to explain this kind of product loyalty, which seems to be based on image rather than tangible product attributes.

Often, loyalties result from genuine concerns about product quality. This is especially important in markets for *experience goods*. As the name suggests, consumers learn about the quality of experience goods by trying them. If consumers care about quality and cannot easily gauge quality without making a purchase, then they will tend to favor sellers who have performed well in the past. Doctors, lawyers, hair stylists, and many other professionals enjoy the benefits of selling experience goods; they can charge prices well in excess of their costs yet retain most of their clients. Likewise, auto manufacturers and even auto insurers thrive because many of their satisfied customers are reluctant to shop around for lower prices, fearful that they could end up with substandard quality. Most goods and services are experience goods, and their sellers enjoy the benefits of softer price competition.

Consumer loyalty in these markets can be challenged when an independent organization publishes quality ratings. Armed with these ratings, consumers are emboldened to shop around, confident that they can identify other high quality sellers. This lesson was learned the hard way by the big three U.S. automakers (General Motors, Ford, and Chrysler), who dominated the domestic market through the 1960s through a combination of brand loyalty, minimal price competition, and a general perception that imported cars had inferior quality. The big three could hold off the imports as long as one of two conditions was met:

1. The perception of superior domestic quality was a reality.
2. The perception was wrong, but consumers did not know it.

By the 1970s, both conditions had broken down. Thanks to innovative manufacturing techniques, the Japanese made better quality cars, and magazines such as *Consumer Reports* began to take notice. Within a decade, Hondas, Toyotas, and Nissans filled U.S. garages.

U.S. doctors have long enjoyed the benefits of selling what is perhaps the quintessential experience good. Most doctors have the luxury of a loyal patient base. This may soon change, thanks to a burgeoning health care report cards movement. Patients who discover that their favorite provider has a high mortality rate might prefer to place their lives in other hands. (To paraphrase television's Doctor House, they may prefer a doctor who cures them to a doctor who likes them.) Doctors who have banked on a good bedside manner to keep a thriving practice may soon find themselves at a competitive disadvantage.

Managers can readily predict when price competition in experience goods markets is likely to be soft. Soft competition is likely when:

- Consumers have little information about the product, and either of the next two points apply.
- The firm's brand is a symbol of quality, while other firms do not share the same brand reputation. Brand is particularly sticky when

the share of the good as a fraction of the consumer's overall budget is small; hence it is hardly worth the customer's while to contemplate if the premium is valid. The customer is likely to just grab the item off the aisle and move on.

- The good is an experience good, and there is no widely disseminated consumer report card. Firms that have high overall quality, or meet unique customer needs, should embrace report cards. Those that thrive on consumer ignorance, rather than value creation, will be the losers. Consumers will pay a premium for experience goods whose quality materially impacts the quality of the consumers' (or their loved ones') lives (as is the case in medical care).

The key implication for managers: By *meeting customer needs in experience goods* markets, you will do more than build market share. You will also soften price competition, assuring higher profit margins. Taken together, high shares and high margins guarantee very high profits.

Unilateral Actions: Building Loyalty through Switching Costs

Sometimes, consumers remain with a seller who increases price because they do not know where else to turn or have to bear a substantial expense to switch. In either case, we say that consumers face *switching costs*. Switching costs appear in many guises. Sometimes, buyers develop brand-specific know-how that is not fully transferable to substitute brands. For example, there are many high-quality personal digital assistants (PDAs), but someone who has taken the time to learn and enter data into a PalmPilot would be reluctant to switch to a Handspring, even if the latter costs less. Product incompatibility softens price competition among competing PDA brands. Sometimes, the seller develops specific know-how about the buyer, such as when a commercial banker develops extensive knowledge of a client's business. This again discourages consumers from shopping around and softens competition.

Frequent Customer Programs

Sellers can also increase switching costs by offering coupons or frequent-customer points that tie discounts or special offerings to the completion of a series of transactions. Everyone is familiar with airline frequent flier programs. Restaurants, car washes, department stores, and even some law firms are among other businesses that use similar loyalty programs. To be successful, the value of loyalty awards must grow at an increasing rate, as shown in Figure 6.2. Otherwise, customers will have no reason to stay with the same program and may even find it worthwhile to diversify their purchases across many sellers. The result is that it can be increasingly costly to maintain the loyalty of the best customers. Airline reward programs very clearly display the pattern shown in Figure 6.2. Fliers remain loyal to a single carrier until they have saved up enough points to win free overseas trips; first class cabins in transoceanic flights are often filled with frequent fliers flying free. This creates a nice scale economy for a carrier in its hub city. Its loyalty program offers

Figure 6.2
To Be Effective, Frequent Customer Awards Must Increase at an Increasing Rate

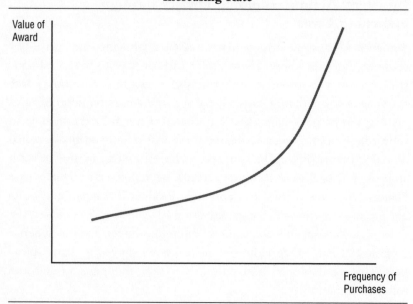

more opportunities to build miles, gives the flier more reward options, and so becomes the program of choice in the market.

Another feature of the best frequent customer programs is that the rewards have low production costs relative to their market value. This is certainly true for airlines, where the cost of filling an empty seat is nearly zero. Airlines are careful to use blackout periods and other restrictions to make sure that a frequent flier flying free does not displace a full fare paying passenger. A related example is the 2004 Focus and a Dell program in which customers who purchased a Ford Focus obtained a free Dell computer. Though not a frequent customer program, the choice of a Dell computer is appropriate because the value is much higher than the marginal cost of production. Children's toys would make bad awards. They would probably be redeemed around Christmas time, just when manufacturers and distributors are at capacity. The marginal cost of filling these awards would be very high.

Some frequent customer programs fail because they target the wrong customers. Frequent customers are usually loyal customers, with or without financial inducements. If anything, sellers should offer better deals to customers who are still on the fence and for whom price still matters. In fact, frequent customer programs work best when most business comes from fence sitters. But remember, the purpose of these programs is not merely to drum up more sales; firms can lower prices to do this. Markets with many fence sitting customers tend to experience intense price competition. By turning fickle customers into loyal customers, firms can soften price competition.

Again, airline frequent flier plans get it right. Airlines recognize that there are few inherent sources of differentiation among the carriers. There would be little customer loyalty in the absence of frequent flier programs, especially in the lucrative business travel segment. Not only do mileage programs increase loyalty and soften competition, the cost of filling the awards is near zero. All in all, this is a no-brainer strategy for an otherwise struggling industry.

The bottom line on frequent customer programs:

• They can build loyalty.
• Reward values must increase at an ever faster rate as the point levels increase.

- Target the fence sitters (as noble as it sounds to reward your most loyal customers, they are going to shop from you anyway).
- Choose awards that have low marginal costs relative to perceived value.

Building Switching Costs: The Lego Solution

One more way to increase switching costs is to offer a bundle of complementary products that fit together in a product line. A customer who has purchased one product from the line will naturally seek out others. This strategy is especially popular among childrens' toys; just ask any parent of a child who plays with Legos whether price is a major consideration when making a purchase. The same holds for Brio Trains, Playmobil construction kits, GI Joe, American Girl, and Barbie dolls—all are priced well above costs. The same business tactics have successfully limited price competition in markets for some adult toys. For example, many owners of Harley Davidson motorcycles embrace the Harley lifestyle that not only includes an attitude about transportation, but also includes a willingness to pay $30 for a Harley logo–emblazoned sweatshirt that would have cost $15 without the logo.

Children's clothing designer Garan Inc. tried the interchangeable parts strategy with mixed success. Thirty years ago, Garan developed a strategy based on the premise that young children would like to pick out their own clothes and dress themselves. Garan also understood that children who dress themselves are likely to look as though they had done so in the dark, perhaps pairing up a blue striped top with an orange plaid bottom, or a red checked shirt with purple flowered pants. Garanimals provided a simple solution to this problem. Each separate article of clothing had a hangtag depicting a different animal. Put a zebra top with a zebra bottom and, voila, the clothes are sure to match. Garan reasoned that children could easily match the animals, and the results would please themselves, their parents, and friends.

Garanimals was a clever gimmick that quickly caught on. By the mid-1970s, Garanimals were as popular as Carter's, OshKosh B'Gosh, and other leading names in children's apparel. There was a subtler element to Garan's strategy: Garanimals had built-in switching costs. Parents of Garanimals kids knew that they could easily expand their children's wardrobes by purchasing more outfits with the same animal hangtags. If little Suzie loved her crocodile top and bottom, another pair of crocodiles would give her four mix-and-match possibilities. Even so, by the early 1980s, Garanimals had lost their appeal. Some parents grew tired of the cute designs and merely acceptable product quality. Furthermore, enforcing the proper use of a product sold for children proved to be problematic; some kids preferred to mix crocodiles with zebras, defeating the purpose of the hangtag system. As always, good ideas must be matched by good execution for the firm to achieve lasting success.

A Laundry List of Tactics for Softening Competition

We have identified several steps that firms can take to soften price competition. But what will work for one product may utterly fail for another. Table 6.1 summarizes the tactics we have described.

BE THY BROTHER'S KEEPER

When one firm slashes prices, its rivals usually follow, depressing industry prices and destroying aggregate industry profits. Competitors naturally seek ways to avoid destructive price competition. In principle, the competitors could simply meet and agree not to cut prices. We do not recommend this, for two reasons. First, such commitments are not enforceable; each firm is free to cut its prices, whether or not it says it will do otherwise. More importantly, conspiring to fix prices is a felony offense that has put business executives behind bars.[2]

Former American Airlines CEO Robert Crandall narrowly avoided prison time in an infamous attempt to fix prices. In 1982, American and now-defunct Braniff Airlines were engaged in a damaging price war. Crandall telephoned Braniff CEO Howard Putnam and said: "Raise your g—— fares 20 percent. I'll raise mine the next morning. You'll make more money and I will, too."[3] Putnam refused to go along with the proposed price hike. This was a good thing for both of them. As it turned out, the conversation was taped and the recording was sent to the Department of Justice. Fortunately for Crandall, a conspiracy requires

Table 6.1
Tactics for Softening Price Competition

Market Conditions	Tactic
If the product is to be used repeatedly, with frequent upgrades:	Design the product or service so that consumers derive more benefits with use, or so that you can offer more benefits to consumers as you gain experience with them.
If good/service is an experience good and it is difficult for consumers to comparison shop for quality:	Establish a strong brand identity.
If the good/service is not an experience good, and customers are very price sensitive:	Establish a customer loyalty program, especially if marginal costs are low.
All goods and services:	Offer complementary goods to form a coordinated product line.

two or more parties; without Putnam's cooperation, there was no conspiracy, and Crandall was off the hook.

It should be crystal clear that competitors cannot talk directly to each other about prices. Indirect communication through a third party is no better and only brings more people into the conspiracy. To avoid running afoul of the law, firms must make their pricing decisions unilaterally. In some situations, unilateral price announcements may be enough to soften price competition. Such price leadership is perhaps the best-known example of a *facilitating practice*: a policy that limits the risk of cutthroat price competition. Here are examples of some common facilitating practices.

Price Leadership

Many industries have a *price leader*, a firm that is usually first to announce its price increases. This announcement can have a sentinel effect, with the competition matching the price increase shortly thereafter. If the leader announces prices that maximize *industry profits*, and the followers go along, the result is profit maximization for all. The followers will see little reason to rock the boat, and the facilitating practice can last for years. This seems to describe historical pricing patterns in the breakfast cereal industry. For decades, Kellogg's assumed the role of price leader. Its annual, unilaterally announced price hikes seemed more than adequate to cover increases in production costs and were quickly matched by General Mills, Post, and other big competitors. The industry prospered, but because Kellogg's announcements were unilateral, the industry's pricing practices went unchallenged by federal officials.

Sometimes, firms announce price increases weeks or even months before they will become effective. Preannouncements often help customers plan their future purchases, such as when building suppliers announce price increases during the winter months, allowing contractors to better budget for the spring construction season. But when a preannouncement has no obvious benefit for customers, antitrust agencies are sure to take a close look. In 1992, the U.S. Department of Justice challenged an airline industry practice when carriers announced unilateral price increases a full month before they would become effective. The DOJ pointed out that if competitors did not go along with the price increase, then the carrier could quickly back down without losing appreciable business. This made it easier for the carrier to test the waters, so to speak, making it much easier to lead all carriers to a round of price increases. Most carriers settled the case, agreeing not to preannounce price hikes. When an airline wants to raise prices today, it usually does so on a Friday afternoon. Given that there are relatively few tickets purchased over the weekend (especially for lucrative business travel), Friday afternoon announcements give the carriers two days to see how competitors will respond. Sometimes, competitors do not follow suit, and the price hike is rescinded by Monday morning.

Other Facilitating Practices

There are other industry practices that may facilitate price increases. In the 1960s, General Electric escaped a brutal price war with Westinghouse in the turbine generator market that was caused, in part, by secret pricing and lumpy contracts (recall symptoms 8 and 9 from the previous chapter). Each firm had attempted to increase prices, but these efforts were not verifiable and were met with skepticism by its rival. GE finally overcame Westinghouse's suspicion by publishing its prices and then offering most favored customer status to all of its customers, promising to give each one the lowest price it charged to any of them. GE even hired an accounting firm to enforce this practice. Westinghouse felt certain that GE would not secretly undercut its published prices (doing so with one customer would force GE to give a refund to everyone else) and followed suit. While the breadth of these facilitating practices ultimately resulted in an antitrust action, each individual practice—public pricing, most favored customer status, and pricing audits—may survive scrutiny on its own.

Firms can also facilitate price increases by punishing rivals who do not go along. This can be as simple as matching (or even surpassing) any discounts offered by a rival firm. Again, the airline industry offers a compelling example. During the late 1980s, Chicago-based Midway Airlines entered a number of markets previously dominated by Northwest Airlines. In March 1991, Midway slashed its prices to as low as $29 each way on most flights. Northwest retaliated by reducing its fares at Midway Airport, striking the former where it hurt the most. This surgical counterstrike came at little cost to Northwest, which had a minor presence at Midway Airport. By September, Midway Airlines was nearly bankrupt, and Northwest acquired it a month later. By swiftly punishing upstart price cutters, such tit-for-tat behavior may be the best way to maintain pricing stability. Either the smaller firm rescinds its price cuts, or it runs the risk of bankruptcy.

Tit-for-Tat

It takes more than a savvy price leader for an industry to avoid cutthroat price competition. The followers must be equally savvy, and the price leader must be willing to enforce market discipline if a rival does not go along. The price leader must match its rival's price cuts, or perhaps slash prices even further. The price cuts must be supported by output expansion, so as to win back the share that the rival took away.

The logic behind enforcing market discipline is very simple: If one firm harms its competitors, the competitors must strike back with equal or superior force. This should have a deterrent effect, giving pause to the next would-be price cutter. Be forewarned: Such predatory pricing may run afoul of the antitrust laws, especially if prices are slashed below variable costs.

International government-owned cartels are immune from most antitrust actions. OPEC is the best-known such cartel, and has both a savvy leader and shrewd followers. Led by Saudi Arabia, the largest OPEC members set output quotas so as to reach target prices. When member nations exceed their output targets, the Saudis flood the market with oil, depressing prices and punishing the wayward states. OPEC's success has been threatened in recent years by production from nonmember nations such as Russia. However, nonmembers seem content with low shares and high market prices (as opposed to low shares and low prices), and usually allow the Saudis to establish a world price.

This suggests that there are two keys to successful price leadership:

1. When a firm leads with a price hike, its rivals should follow.
2. If a firm reduces its prices, rivals should do the same.[4]

This is known as *tit-for-tat pricing*. If all firms play tit-for-tat, then the price leader should select the industry monopoly price. Rivals will follow suit, and industry profits will be maximized.

Tit-for-tat works because it encourages each firm to take a long-term view of competition. Strategies that boost short-term profits are short-circuited, because of the tremendous harm that may follow. Table 6.2 presents a game matrix that illustrates the short-term problem, showing the payoffs at stake in a typical competitive battle between two firms. Each firm may select one of two pricing tactics, labeled Passive (try to maintain a high price) and Aggressive (set a low price). The first entry in each cell is Player 1's short run payoff; the second entry is the short run payoff to Player 2. For example, if Player 1 is passive and Player 2 is aggressive, then Player 1 receives $0 and Player 2 receives $100. If Player 1 and Player 2 are both aggressive, then both receive $10.

Table 6.2
Pricing Tactics

		Player 2			
		Aggressive		Passive	
Player 1	Aggressive	$10	$ 10	$100	$ 0
	Passive	$ 0	$100	$ 75	$75

Many readers will recognize this table as an example of a "prisoner's dilemma," one of the foundations of game theory.[5] The data in the table reveal that in the short run, each player may think it pays to be aggressive. This is seen by noting that regardless of what the other player does, each player has a higher payoff if it plays aggressively. Unfortunately for both players, simultaneous aggressive play leaves just $10 apiece, the smallest combined profit.

The prisoner's dilemma has been widely studied by economists and psychologists, often using experimental settings that mimic competitive conditions. Often, researchers have participants play the game one time only so as to create a short-term focus. In these games, most players are aggressive and profits are small. But when participants are asked to compete head to head for 20 repetitions of the game or more, they learn quickly to be passive, with aggressive play appearing only in the final one or two periods (when there is no long run). There have even been Prisoner's Dilemma tournaments, in which contestants submit computer programs with instructions on how to play each period as a function of the game play in prior periods. Players who submit the simple tit-for-tat strategy are invariably among the top performers. They quickly achieve the passive/passive solution, and if their rivals do cheat by playing aggressive, their retaliation soon brings them back in line.

Here are the key takeaways from the tit-for-tat theory and experiments:

- Deterrence can lead to peaceful coexistence.
- If a rival does attack you, respond by inflicting the maximum possible damage for the least amount of pain.

- Strike at markets that the rival dominates but be prepared for similar counterstrikes.
- In time, each firm will learn that by playing tit-for-tat, it can enjoy its share of the spoils and have no incentive to rock the boat.
- Be patient. Rivals may not learn to understand each other's intentions without a few periods of prolonged hostilities.

A Word of Caution

Tactics aimed at softening price competition often harm consumers. Antitrust agencies are well aware of the consequences for consumers of price preannouncements, tit-for-tat, and other facilitating practices. In fact, the large turbine industry, the breakfast cereal industry, and the airline industry have all faced tough scrutiny from the U.S. Department of Justice. Many industry practices have been abandoned as a result of DOJ antitrust actions.

Given the tremendous scrutiny of federal antitrust agencies, managers who are seeking pricing stability should heed the following advice:[6]

- All pricing decisions should be made unilaterally. Avoid all direct contacts with competitors about price.
- It is okay to match a competitor's price reduction. But do not overretaliate. Setting a very low price may be perceived as an attempt to instill pricing discipline.
- Carefully handle public pricing communications.
- Have a legitimate justification for price increases, most favored customer clauses, and pricing audits.[7]
- By the same token, have a legitimate justification for price cuts. "Meeting the competition" is a legitimate justification. There is almost never a legitimate justification for pricing below average variable costs; this is very likely to raise the eyebrows of antitrust enforcers.
- Do not preannounce price increases without a legitimate business justification.

- Limit the audience: Generally it is better to tell customers directly whenever feasible.
- Monitor the content: Announce price changes; do not lecture competitors about the need to raise prices, or the consequences of reducing them.
- Keep analyses of probable competitive reactions private. It is okay to perform such analyses, but it is not okay to share them.
- Finally, do not take the word of economists when there is a strategic aspect to your pricing decisions. Clear your pricing tactics with an attorney well-versed in antitrust law.

DON'T THROW STONES

Even when an industry enjoys facilitating practices such as price leadership and tit-for-tat, some firms may still insist on cutting prices. Firms that have low costs or expect to enjoy a permanent increase in market share from a temporary price cut are likely candidates to disrupt the status quo. Firms may cut prices for other reasons. Some firms may be unaware or willfully ignorant of the strategic implications of their decisions. They reduce prices because they fail to anticipate the competitive response. More sophisticated firms might understand the risks, yet misread or misjudge the competitive situation, causing an accidental flaring up of pricing instability.

Avoiding the Costs of Misreads and Misjudgments

Robert Crandall once reacted to price reductions by then-rival TWA by stating that "an industry is only as smart as its dumbest competitor." He recently made similar comments about price cutting by the latest wave of low fare industry startups. This opinion has been echoed by many of our executive students, who have fallen victim to seemingly dumb pricing tactics by their competitors. Our students often feel that when competitors lower prices, they must immediately respond, lest they embolden the competition to make even deeper cuts. A tit-for-tat price response may be in order, but it can easily trigger an all-out price war. When it comes to competitive pricing, discretion may be advised, at least until the motives of the competition can be ascertained.

The previous chapter described how firms can misread or misjudge a rival's pricing tactics and make an unfortunate leap into a price war. Given the stakes, firms should clearly make every effort to understand rival pricing at a deep level. Even if firms can correctly measure prices, they must also interpret what they mean. Not every price reduction is an act of aggression, and retaliation is not always the best response.

Here are a few steps that firms can do to prevent misreads and misjudgments. Some of these steps may exacerbate other symptoms of price competition, so they should be pursued only if misreads and misjudgments have become a serious concern.

- Standardize the product. This makes it easier for each firm to track its rivals.
- Open pricing. If prices are public, there is less uncertainty about why market shares are shifting.
- Communicate market share expectations. Do not let your rival be surprised by a shift in market share.
- Share demand forecasts. Firms with overly optimistic demand forecasts may blame their rivals for shortfalls.
- Be *forgiving*. Do not be quick to judge your rivals' actions, for reasons we now explain.

Forgiving Tit-for-Tat

Tit-for-tat strategies call for immediate retaliation against price cutters. If misreads and misjudgments are possible, firms that play tit-for-tat run the risk of retaliating to nonexistent threats. The way to avoid the risks of misreads and misjudgments is both simple and frustrating. Be forgiving. If a rival appears to have stolen market share or reduced its price, be patient. It may be better to suffer losses for a few days or weeks, than to trigger a price war that may take months or years to unwind. (Of course, your willingness to forgive will decrease to the extent that the rival's price reduction has stolen your market share.)

If you are forgiving but eventually determine that a rival has made an aggressive bid for market share, then your response must be even more aggressive than mere tit-for-tat. Slash prices even further. If possible, attack the rival's strength (a la Northwest Airlines price cuts at Midway Airport). We have made this point several times in this chapter but it bears repeating: *Maintaining contact in multiple markets* can facilitate precise retaliation and serve as the ultimate deterrence.

"HE WHO LAUGHS LAST LAUGHS BEST," OR "THE ONLY WINNING MOVE IS NOT TO PLAY"

Business school faculty like to play the following game with their students. The professor announces an auction in which the highest bidding student wins $20. There is a hitch: Bidding must occur in $1 increments and both the highest *and second highest* bidders pay what they bid. Invariably, a few students take the bait and start bidding. The class enjoys the excitement, anticipating that a mate will make a quick buck at the professor's expense. The bids quickly reach $10, and then surpass $20! The mood in the class changes, as the two highest bidders realize they have been suckered into a dangerous game and their classmates wonder how high the bidding will go. Eventually, the auction ends, the losing bidder is out a bundle, and even the winning bidder ends up owing the professor.

The game is rigged to favor the professor. To see why, let's work through a typical auction. We will call the two highest bidders Michael and Daniel.[8] Suppose that Michael has just bid $11, topping Daniel's bid of $10. If the bidding stops now, Michael will win $9, and Daniel will lose $10. The professor is already assured of a profit and the students an aggregate loss. Daniel has no desire to come out on the short end, so he ups his bid to $12. Facing a loss of $11 if he backs out, Michael bids $13. The bidding continues unabated. Soon, Michael bids $19. If Daniel drops out, he will lose $18. Instead, he bids $20, even though this guarantees he can do no better than break even. The bidding is still not over.

Michael and Daniel soldier on, each hoping the other will drop out first. As the bidding passes $30, $40, and beyond, Michael and Daniel rue the moment they started bidding.

Michael and Daniel have fallen victim to a *war of attrition*, where each hopes to outlast the other, not to win, but to minimize losses. History tells the story of many such wars of attrition: In World War I, the British and French faced off against the Germans in the trenches of the western front, losing millions of men in futile battles to capture the no-man's land between them; during the post–World War II cold war, the United States and Soviet Union stockpiled nuclear weapons to deter each other from a first strike. In each of these cases, the winners paid a mighty toll, and may have preferred avoiding the battle altogether.

Price wars are wars of attrition. Competitors lose money as margins shrink to a fraction of their original levels. Like Michael and Daniel, their losses mount as the price war continues. The price war will continue until one firm voluntarily exits, is driven into bankruptcy, or raises its prices (and the other goes along). In any event, if the price war lasts too long, even the winning firm may end up losing, unable to make up for the losses incurred in the heat of battle.

The NORAD computer in *WarGames* (recall the discussion in Chapter 5) had a message for parents and children fatigued by the cold war and the arms race war of attrition: "The only winning move is not to play." This would seem to apply to all wars of attrition. But there are some problems with this advice.

- It requires coordination. Businesses cannot openly agree to avoid price wars, and the United States and Soviet Union learned how difficult it was to enforce agreements not to expand nuclear stockpiles.
- If one firm believes the other will not join a war of attrition, it has an incentive to be aggressive and launch a first strike, whether by initiating price cutting or shooting missiles.
- This advice is useless once the war of attrition has begun. In those situations, firms need to know how to win.

Winning the War of Attrition—He Who Loses the Least, Wins the Most

Suppose our professor tweaks the auction just a little bit. The rules for Michael remain the same, but Daniel has to pay $.50 every time he bids. Forced to pay more to remain in the war of attrition, Daniel is likely to drop out rather quickly. Knowing this, Michael is likely to hold fast in his bidding. In the context of business, firms with higher costs should avoid getting trapped in price wars. Not only do they suffer more during the war, but if their rivals know this, it will encourage them to continue. Wal-Mart subsidiary Sam's Club leveraged its cost advantage to win a late-1990s price war with Pace, Price Company, and Costco in the warehouse club retailing market. This price war was so brutal that staff at Sam's Club rivals used to purchase merchandise from Sam's Club, repackage it, and then resell it at their own stores! But Sam's Club's rivals could not match its costs and eventually retreated, either going bankrupt or avoiding further head-to-head battles in Sam's Club markets.

The general point is that some firms lose more than others during a war of attrition. The firms with the most to lose are likely to be the first to try to end the war. This suggests that the relationship between size and staying power may be rather unexpected; bigger firms may want to drop out sooner, so as to avoid large losses. In markets for commodity goods, for example, the biggest firms have the greatest incentive to cut production, stabilize prices, and reap the potentially enormous benefits of pricing stability. This has a profound impact on strategies in declining markets. Once demand falls, prices may plummet. Rather than wait while profits hemorrhage, larger firms may want to cut production as soon as they are sure demand is not soon likely to recover.

Because of this size asymmetry, many wars of attrition follow a predictable path. A large incumbent is threatened by an upstart firm intent on securing its place in the market. Both dig in their heels. As losses pile up at the larger firm, it takes action to end the war of attrition. The AFL/NFL bidding war described in the previous chapter is a good example. As players' salaries soared, the larger NFL bore the brunt of the increase. The NFL ultimately gave in, agreeing to a merger under conditions that favored the new league.

In the early 1990s, a war of attrition broke out in the British satellite television business, with similar results.[9] A few years before the battle had begun, a business consortium in the United Kingdom launched two satellites into space, setting the stage for British Satellite Broadcasting (BSB). BSB was the UK's first satellite television company. BSB planned to begin broadcasts in 1989, and hoped to have 5 million customers by 2003. These hopes were dashed when Rupert Murdoch's News Corps launched a competitor called Sky Television. Sky TV used an older, less powerful satellite that required less costly home satellite dishes. It also tended to have cheaper programming. Together, the two companies invested more than £1 billion pounds in startup costs, with Sky TV positioned as the smaller, but less costly competitor.

With its older technology, Sky TV made it to the market first while BSB encountered several technological glitches. By 1990, however, both companies were competing for customers. Competition occurred on three dimensions: price, marketing expenditures, and programming costs. Price competition was limited to things like free trial periods, but neither firm raised price to meet their higher than expected operating costs. Both BSB and Sky TV spent much more than expected on marketing both to consumers and electronics retailers. Most problematically, BSB and Sky TV locked horns in a bidding war to obtain exclusive rights to popular movies. In this battle, combined programming fees quickly mushroomed to £20 million a month. At the depths of the war of attrition, the two companies were losing a combined £10 million per week. With its higher cost structure, BSB bore the lion's share of the losses. In November 1990, the war of attrition abruptly ended, when BSB and Sky merged under conditions very favorable to Sky.

Winning the War of Attrition—Deep Pockets and Commitment

In the AFL/NFL and BSB/Sky TV wars of attrition, the upstarts won. This seems counterintuitive; we normally expect bigger firms to survive. This expectation is due to the familiar deep pockets theory: We believe that the firm with the deeper pockets will outlast its rivals. The rivals know this, so they pull out before suffering too much. There is a lot of merit to this theory, and either Michael or Daniel could have used it to his advantage in the $20 auction. Suppose that Daniel visited an Automated Teller Machine prior to class and withdrew $300. When the bidding began, he could show off his big pile of money. Figuring there is no way he could outbid Daniel, Michael (and the rest of the class) would quickly drop out.

Daniel's deep pockets strategy is not without risks. It is absolutely essential that his classmates know about Daniel's stash of cash. If Michael has equal piles of cash and is equally stubborn, the losses can be staggering. Deep pockets may help a firm win a war of attrition, or they may increase the losses.

Deep pockets can be an advantage, but only if they scare rivals into submission. There are other ways to achieve the same effect. In the $20 auction, Daniel would like to convince Michael that he will not be outbid. He could adopt the following strategy: He gives his money to a classmate, whom he authorizes to place bids. Moreover, he promises to give the classmate $10 if he wins the bidding, regardless of the final price. He makes all of this public. Michael knows he is beat. This designated bidder has only one goal, and that is to win. Michael figures he had better not even start the bidding. Daniel wins the auction, for a bid of $1.

Daniel's strategy represents a *public commitment to winning*. Firms can demonstrate a similar commitment to winning. They can invest in productive capacity, effectively reducing the incremental costs to the point where it actually pays to keep producing. Along these lines, they can sign long term labor contracts that cannot be voided. Forced to pay labor whether they produce or not, they may as well stay open for business. Rivals know this and back down. Or they can give their managers pay-for-performance deals that reward market share gains rather than profits. In all cases, they need to publicly announce their commitments.

Just the appearance of a commitment may be sufficient to win. Some firms, such as Occidental Petroleum, gained fame for seemingly enjoying price wars, no matter the cost. When firms have this sort of reputation for toughness, their rivals will think twice about instigating a price war. Perhaps this was on President Ronald Reagan's mind when he suggested that the United States could survive a nuclear war. In the real world of War Games, such an astonishing statement might have given the Soviets pause about their ability to outlast the United States in the event of such a global catastrophe.

Losing the War of Attrition: Knowing When to Fold 'Em

What happens when both firms are committed to winning? The war of attrition starts to resemble a game of poker, but with much higher stakes. When playing the game, managers must remember the basic rules:

- If you are sustaining greater short term losses than your rival, you should give up first. If your rival knows you are sustaining greater losses, you have even more reason to get out.
- Firms that demonstrate greater tangible commitments are more likely to win.

Price wars and other wars of attrition require delicate yet crucial managerial decisions. As difficult as it is to sustain losses during a battle that cannot be won, it is even more difficult to downsize or exit from a market and then look back in hindsight to wonder if the firm gave up prematurely.

WRAP-UP: AN OVERVIEW OF STRATEGIC PRICING

This chapter presents a variety of tactics that firms can adopt to soften price competition. Table 6.3 provides a handy summary.

Table 6.3
Softening Price Competition

Theme	Comments
An Ounce of Prevention Is Worth a Pound of Cure	• Target narrow segments to limit the number of competitors. • Imprint a strong brand reputation on experience goods, especially when there is no independent shopping guide. • Create switching costs by developing customer specific knowledge, having the customer develop product specific knowledge, or assembling a collection of interrelated products. • Create frequent customer programs that target fence sitting customers.
Be Thy Brother's Keeper	• Never openly discuss prices with competitors, or via intermediaries. • Allow one firm to take the lead in announcing annual price changes; competitors can follow suit, thereby minimizing the risk of price wars. • Granting most favored customer status may placate large purchasers, but it also softens price competition. • Practice tit-for-tat pricing to restore a sense of trust among competitors. • Consult with an attorney before taking any strategic decisions designed to raise industry prices.
Do Not Throw Stones	• "An industry is only as smart as its stupidest competitor." Take stock of who that is, and be prepared to act. • Be aware of the conditions that foster misreads and misjudgments, and be forgiving when those conditions are present.
He Who Laughs Last Laughs Best	• Avoid wars of attrition unless you are confident of a decisive victory. • If your firm is losing more each day the price war endures, you should raise prices or reduce output first. If your rival is losing more each day, hold on tight and pray it comes to its senses. • If you can, make credible commitments to stay in. This should encourage your rival to bow out.

NOTES

1. A. Brandenberger and B. Nalebuff, *Coopetition*, New York: Doubleday, 1996.

2. The law was apparently no deterrent to senior executives at food giant Archer Daniels Midland (ADM), who conspired with several Japanese competitors to fix the prices of lysine and citric acid. Unfortunately for ADM, a high-level manager who participated in these conspiratorial discussions was an FBI mole who wore a hidden microphone to several meetings in which price fixing and other collusive arrangements were discussed. The recordings were enough to put ADM's CEO and a division president into federal prison.

3. Taken from www.mhhe.com/economics/mcconnell15e/student/olc/chap32analogies.mhtml. Viewed on 7/20/2004.

4. Firms may need to reduce prices even further, so as to punish the firm that cut prices first. This is especially important if the initial firm stands to gain, long term, from its pricing strategy.

5. A prisoner's dilemma occurs whenever the selfish actions of each participant result in a poor collective outcome.

6. Some of these suggestions are from J. Kessler and R. Wheeler, *Antitrust* (Summer 1993): pp. 26–29, "An old theory gets new life: How to price without being a 'price signaler.' "

7. These are sometimes demanded by powerful purchasers. Antitrust law suggests that sellers will not be challenged for agreeing to such demands. Economic theory suggests that this can actually benefit the seller, because it tends to increase prices to less powerful purchasers.

8. Any resemblance to Professor Dranove's sons' names is coincidence, though there are times when the professor would like to try this game out on them.

9. Some of the information for this example was taken from "Sky Television versus British Satellite Broadcasting," HBS Case 9-792-039, and P. Ghemawat, *Games Businesses Play*, Cambridge, MA; MIT Press, 1997.

CHAPTER 7

THE THREAT OF ENTRY AND HOW TO COMBAT IT

Thus far, we have described what it takes for firms to outperform their rivals and avoid the ravages of competition. Firms that do both will enjoy superior profits in the short run. But many successful firms find it difficult to sustain their performance. This chapter discusses one of the most important obstacles to enduring profits: the threat of entry. The next chapter examines a broad class of obstacles known collectively as *isolating mechanisms*.

There is a seemingly endless list of profitable firms that have been toppled by entrants. Motorola, once supreme in the cellular phone market, was usurped by Nokia, which is now threatened by Samsung. Crown Books thought it had a stranglehold on the discount book market until Amazon offered a less costly and more convenient alternative way to shop. Japanese electronics companies dominated the digital television market until South Korean competitors introduced plasma and digital light processing technologies. Not every successful firm has yielded to newcomers, of course. Coke and Pepsi have beaten back upstart cola makers (and "uncola" makers) for the better part of the past 100 years. Kids have been playing with Lego blocks for more than 70 years. In the rapidly evolving world of technology, Palm remains the leading seller of PDAs, despite an onslaught of challengers.

It is difficult to find a successful firm that has not been challenged by entrants. In this chapter, we explain why some firms are able to weather the threat of entry better than others. Managers armed with

155

this knowledge will be able to assess whether their firms are positioned to withstand entry, and if not, what they can do about it.

A remarkable research study offers some sobering facts about the threat posed by entry.[1] Bear in mind that the study is nearly 20 years old and the threat of entry has likely increased due to globalization and stronger capital markets. Here are the key implications of the study. Suppose your firm is making a strategic plan for the next five years. You should expect that 30 percent to 40 percent of your competitors five years hence will be entrants. Most will be greenfield entrants that do not exist at all today; a few will be established firms diversifying from other markets. Within five years, these newcomers will grab 15 percent to 20 percent of the market share. One or two may grow to match your own market share. Although there is considerable variation in entry across industries (for reasons we discuss later), the main takeaway applies nearly everywhere: Your strategic plan must explicitly address the likelihood of entry.

If you are going to anticipate entry, you must put yourself in the shoes of a potential entrant. What are the best markets for the entrants to target? Will they enter specific geographic markets, fill specific product niches, or introduce a lower cost alternative? Once you have identified these opportunities, try to assess the profitability of different entry strategies. Will profits in a specific segment exceed the hurdle rate that is likely to be required for the commensurate investments? Be certain that if you can identify a profitable entry opportunity, others will have already done so, and the potential for entry will soon become a reality.

ENTRY, SUNK COSTS, AND ASYMMETRIES

Analysis of entry opportunities usually involves comparing rates of return against hurdle rates, or computing a net present value (NPV) for the entry decision. Ideally, NPV analysis should account for the many uncertainties about demand, costs, and competition that arise and are resolved as markets unfold. Financial economists have recently shown how to apply mathematical models from finance to entry analysis, allowing strategists to fully account for these complexities. The appendix to this chapter introduces this approach, known as real options theory.

A key finding from real options theory is that it is wrong to base any sunk investment decision on NPV analysis, including the decision to enter a market. Here is an example of how NPV can be misleading. Typically a firm can choose when to sink an investment. Suppose that the investment has a positive NPV: By the standard NPV > 0 criterion, the firm should make the investment. But suppose that as time elapses, the firm learns information about the value of the investment (e.g., it learns that the market demand has changed). By waiting and learning, the firm is better able to avoid sinking the investment in bad times. There is an "option value of waiting" because valuable information is revealed over time. Since NPV ignores the issue of timing of the project, the NPV > 0 criterion leads to overinvestment. On the other hand, if sinking an investment today opens up new opportunities in the future—sometimes known as "add-on opportunities"—then there is value to proceeding even if NPV is slightly negative.

The general point is that the start date of a project can materially affect its value. If by waiting critical information is revealed, then the option value of waiting is likely to be quite high. If by proceeding an important early-mover advantage is secured, then the option value of proceeding is likely high. It is worth considering how the wait and add-on options might enter into determining the value of an entry decision.

Sunk Costs and Asymmetries

Both the traditional NPV approach and the real options approach to entry analysis build off the same fundamentals. The analyst compares *expected postentry earnings* (i.e., the profits enjoyed after the firm enters the market) against *sunk entry costs* (i.e., the nonrecoverable costs associated with entry). Postentry earnings are shaped by the fundamentals of market demand, the firm's strategic position, and the competitive environment. The basic tools spelled out earlier in the book—the resources and capabilities and the strategic analysis checklist—are essential for forecasting future earnings.

Thus far, we have said rather little about sunk costs. One of the most common mistakes in strategy is to equate sunk costs with fixed costs. They are not the same, because fixed costs are often recoverable. Airlines provide a classic example of the distinction between fixed and sunk costs. It might seem to be terrifically expensive to launch a new carrier. Even small passenger jet planes sell for upward of $50 million, and a new airline must also secure airport gates. Most of these costs are not sunk, however. If the airline fails, it can sell its planes and gates to another carrier. An entrant does not even have to purchase its own planes and gates; it can lease them. (At any given time, there are more than 100 Boeing 737s available for lease at prices as low as $50,000 per month.)[2] The sunk cost of starting a new airline is much less than one might initially guess.

The distinction between sunk and fixed costs is essential to understanding the strategic differences between incumbent firms and newcomers. Consider airlines again. If a failed newcomer can sell its planes for close to the purchase price, so, too, can established carriers. The same goes for gates and even landing rights. When it comes to these costs of doing business, there is little meaningful distinction between incumbents and newcomers. If these were the only costs of doing business, then incumbents and newcomers could exchange places almost willy-nilly, ATA could become United Airlines overnight, and vice versa.

Such a reversal is impossible to imagine, of course, so we need to figure out what makes ATA and United different. In general, incumbents and entrants differ from one another because of *asymmetries*. Sometimes, the asymmetries really are as simple as sunk costs that the incumbent has incurred but the entrant has not. For example, Boeing and Airbus are protected from entry by other potential manufacturers of large commercial aviation airframes because they have already made hundreds of millions of dollars of sunk investments in construction facilities, tools, and training. These would represent incremental costs, rather than sunk costs, to a newcomer.

Asymmetries also arise from relationships with customers and suppliers that can take years to build. Over the course of decades, United Airlines established good customer relationships with millions of Mileage Plus travelers, its own employees, government agencies, and Star Alliance partners. United also has learned how to manage a complex hub-and-spoke system. These relationships and knowledge are somewhat specific to Chicago, Denver, and its other hub cities. ATA could eventually establish the same relationships, but this would take time, during which it would suffer millions of dollars in losses. It is the *adjustment costs* associated with trying to match United's relationships and knowledge, rather than any fixed costs of operating an airline, that protect incumbents like United. From United's point of view, these costs are sunk. But a new carrier has yet to incur them; this asymmetry is the major obstacle to entry. Of course, United can easily destroy these relationships; this is a major challenge as it attempts to emerge from bankruptcy. If it fails this challenge, it will lose much of the advantage it enjoys over upstart firms and will become highly vulnerable to entry.

Asymmetries can also arise when it is costly for a consumer to switch from one seller to another. Prior to 2004, cellular phone users could not keep their phone numbers when switching to a new provider. This served as a barrier to newcomers trying to sign up customers of incumbent firms. Thus, the switching costs that can soften competition among incumbent rivals (recall Chapter 6) can also serve to protect those rivals from entry.

Remember, it is asymmetries that distinguish incumbents from entrants. Asymmetries can arise from:

- Sunk investments in facilities, tools, and dyes that cannot be resold on the open market.
- Worker training that is not easily transferable.
- Relationships with customers, suppliers, and employees.
- Switching costs.

Your strategic analysis of entry must consider the extent to which your firm is protected by these asymmetries.

Sunk Costs and Entry in the MRI Market

The distinction between fixed costs and sunk costs, and the associated concept of asymmetries, helps explain the remarkable growth, decline, and rebirth of the market for magnetic resonance imaging (MRI). At a price of $2 million or more for a new magnetic imaging machine, it would seem prohibitively costly for a physician to provide

MRI services, leaving the market to large hospitals with greater financial wherewithal. But there is a thriving aftermarket for MRIs, and a physician who wants to get out of the MRI business can recover most of the purchase price. In fact, physicians do not have to buy an MRI machine. Major manufacturers such as Siemens and General Electric lease new MRIs, and resellers lease used ones at even lower prices.

Leasing has a profound impact on the market for providing MRI services. Physicians can start an MRI practice with a brand new $2 million machine while risking only a fraction of this amount. (Some of the cost of designing and building a dedicated MRI facility is sunk, but only to the extent that it is costly to redesign the facility for another purpose.) The results are predictable. Back in the 1980s, when MRI technology first emerged, insurers often paid physicians more than $1,000 per procedure. With virtually zero marginal costs, this was too good an opportunity for physicians to pass up, and hundreds of them entered the business of selling MRI services. By the early 1990s, there was a glut of physician-owned MRI facilities.

For a while, prices for MRIs held firm, as referring physicians and their insured patients tended to ignore prices when selecting an MRI provider. But it was at this time that managed care organizations began to flourish. These insurers held down medical costs by negotiating discounts from health care providers. MRI providers were not exempt from this exercise of purchasing power, and prices for MRIs fell by more than half. There were few asymmetries to protect incumbents, and insurers often directed patients to the lowest price provider. This put entrants and incumbents on a level playing field. Many MRI providers—incumbents and newcomers alike—exited the market and both GE and Siemens had to take back their leased machines.

If any erred during this period of boom and bust, it was GE and Siemens. The two dominated the MRI market, yet did a poor job of managing the value chain. By virtually eliminating sunk entry costs, they precipitated the resulting price war among physicians. Had GE and Siemens limited leasing, they would have assured handsome profits throughout the value chain and could have set leasing prices to make sure they received their fair share.

Thanks to many new applications of MRI technology, the demand for MRIs is at an all-time high. This time, GE and Siemens lack the power to control the market, as competition from the likes of Toshiba and Philips assures that no one or two firms can limit supply. Leases and resales of used equipment are widespread, and there are more physicians in the MRI market than ever before. The power of managed care organizations has weakened since the 1990s, however, as patients have demanded the freedom to choose their own providers. Insurers lack the strength to negotiate deep discounts, and incumbent MRI providers are relying on established referral patterns to give them an edge over entrants. For the time being, established MRI providers are enjoying healthy profits, even as competition has eroded the profits of MRI manufacturers.

DETERRING ENTRY

A combination of high profits, low sunk costs, and minimal asymmetries invites entry. Managers of incumbent firms might wonder what they can do to deter it. Some entry deterring tactics require firms to depart from their usual business practices and sacrifice short-term profits. These include limit pricing, predatory pricing, and holding excess capacity, all of which we describe later. Before incumbents take such rash steps, they should determine whether entry deterrence is both possible and necessary.

Sometimes, the entrant's expected discounted postentry earnings exceed the sunk costs of entry by such a large amount that it is going to enter no matter what the incumbents do. Economist Joseph Bain described this situation as one of *accommodated entry*, where the incumbent is better off preparing to compete with entrants rather than wasting resources in a futile effort to keep them out.[3] From the physician's point of view, the market for MRI services accommodates entry, and it would be pointless for any one physician to attempt to deter entry by others. The DVD hardware market in the early 2000s also accommodated entry. As much as Sony, Toshiba, and the other major players wanted to deter entry, the market was too profitable and growing too rapidly to deter entry by Apex, Bravo, and other low price brands.

At other times, the potential for an entrant to turn a profit is bleak, and entry does not occur under any circumstances. Bain described this situation as one of *blockaded entry*. Entry is often blockaded because of limited market potential, such as when a market is large enough to support one firm but not two. Firms seeking to penetrate virgin markets would do well to enter those that will subsequently be blockaded due to their limited size. Wal-Mart has used this strategy with great success, opening stores in markets like Juneau, Alaska. With a metropolitan area of around 30,000, Juneau is not large enough to support a second mass merchandiser; Wal-Mart has the market all to itself. Southwest Airlines chooses many of its origin–destination pairs with the same eye toward blockading entry. Remember, limited market potential is not enough; the market must be small relative to the sunk costs of entry. Likewise, even large markets may be blockaded if sunk entry costs are large.

Many other factors can blockade entry. Incumbents may hold protective patents or copyrights, though the amount of protection these afford varies considerably by country. Incumbents may control essential resources, as DeBeers has done in the diamond trade. Whatever the reason for blockaded entry, there is no reason for an incumbent to pursue aggressive entry deterring strategies in blockaded markets.

Access to Distribution Channels

Limited access to distribution channels often serves as a long-lived entry deterrent, especially in consumer product markets. Incumbents tie up channels (often through long term contracts or strong vendor relationships), and entrants struggle to find access to consumers. Often, the owners of the channels stand to prosper the most from exclusivity deals, but the terms of the contracts usually assure that the incumbents supplying to the channels share in the spoils. In any event, entrants are squeezed out.

The breakfast cereal market has experienced one of the longest and most highly publicized disputes about channel access, one that is still ongoing. Take a close look at the breakfast cereal aisle in your grocery store. More than likely you will find that a small number of major cereal makers (Kellogg's, General Foods, Post) dominate the offerings, with seemingly every possible combination and permutation of flakes, fruits, and nuts. While consumers benefit from variety, many industry observers argue that this product proliferation ties up all the available shelf space, making it impossible for other companies to get their products on the shelves.

When combined with the pricing stability once afforded by Kellogg's price leadership that we described in Chapter 6, such entry deterrence was a potent force for sustained profitability. Indeed, breakfast cereal makers were among the most profitable U.S. companies for much of the past century. In the 1970s, the Federal Trade Commission (FTC) filed a complaint against cereal makers, alleging that brand proliferation harmed consumers by denying competitors access to store shelves. The case was not a slam dunk for the FTC, as the cereal makers offered legitimate business justifications for proliferation (such as satisfying the American consumer's taste for variety), and there were other potential outlets for competing cereals (like Wal-Mart). After a prolonged trial, the FTC dropped the case in the 1980s.

The tobacco industry enjoyed a similar confluence of circumstances. Historically, cigarettes were sold in one of three venues: grocery stores (at the checkout counter), vending machines, and bars. This retail space was limited, and product proliferation meant that upstart brands had few opportunities to penetrate mainstream channels. The industry leaders also enjoyed a long history of soft price competition, due in part to strong brand loyalty, not to mention the erstwhile competitors' historic association in the American Tobacco Trust. In any event, the combination of soft price competition and entry barriers guaranteed high profits.

Asymmetries are essential to maintaining the entry barrier. After all, newcomers can outbid incumbents for channel access. Incumbents must have some advantage other than mere incumbency if they are to assure themselves of superior access; a superior B–C position would certainly help. In some cases, the mere specter of upstream competition may be enough to convince the channels to favor the incumbents. After all, Kellogg's could not pay hefty slotting fees if competition in the cereal market eroded most of Kellogg's profits. No matter what, the incumbent must share its spoils with the channel.

If limiting access to channels helps incumbents enjoy high profits, it stands to reason that opening of new channels is a major threat to profitability. By the mid-1990s, both breakfast cereal and cigarette makers faced this threat. The culprit in both cases was the rapid growth of mass merchandisers. By the mid-1990s, Wal-Mart and Target were among the nation's leading retailers in both product categories and were happy to sell off-brand products favored by many of their price-sensitive customers.

Leading brand name manufacturers in both industries responded to the new threats in the same way, by slashing prices. The price war initiated by Philip Morris in early 1993 helped hasten the exit of some new cigarette makers to the market, but it also hurt industry profits and cut stock market valuations of tobacco companies nearly in half. A similar price war broke out in the cereal market in 1996, with similar results for entrants and incumbents. While neither industry has recovered, it is not clear if anyone is to blame for the decline in profits. The threat of entry was like a powder keg. When mass merchandisers broke the stranglehold on access that had protected incumbents for many decades, it lit a fuse under the competition that could not be put out.

Limit Pricing

If the market is too attractive to deter entry, incumbents might want to make the market seem less attractive. One way to do this may be to lower prices, a tactic known as *limit pricing*. Here is an example of why limit pricing might work. Consider the following choice:

- Your firm enjoys a 100 percent market share with 30 percent profit margins forever.
- Your firm enjoys a 100 percent market share with 50 percent margins for one year, and 50 percent market share with 30 percent margins thereafter.

At any discount rate below 50 percent, the first option is more attractive. Limit pricing can make it happen. The logic of limit pricing is that by reducing price below monopoly levels, the successful incumbent can make the market appear slightly less attractive to potential entrants. The incumbent has a slightly lower profit margin, but never experiences entry. The logic is so compelling that according to one survey, nearly half of all managers with pricing responsibilities have engaged in limit pricing.[4]

Despite its intuitive appeal and widespread use, there is no systematic theoretical or empirical evidence that limit pricing actually deters entry. Unlike obtaining a patent or tying up a distribution channel, limit pricing does not create any technical barriers to entry. It only works if it changes the *attitudes* of potential entrants about the potential for postentry earnings. Thus, any consideration of limit pricing must consider the psychological impact on potential entrants.

Potential entrants must have some idea of the potential size of the market and the price that a monopolist firm ought to charge. So the relevant question is: What would potential entrants think if the monopolist price was less than what they expected? Perhaps they would reconsider their estimates of the market size. If the incumbent can convince the entrants that the market is not very large, the entrants may stay out. Or perhaps the limit price will convince entrants that the incumbent is very efficient and actually prospers at a low price point. Postentry competition might therefore destroy the entrant. Another possibility is that limit pricing signals the incumbent's intention to fight tooth and nail to hold onto its market share in the event of entry. Such signals can be highly effective, provided the incumbent has not given entrants reasons to believe it will be accommodating if push comes to shove and entry does occur.

As always, asymmetries are critical to entry deterrence. If entrants are privy to solid market research or know the incumbent's actual sales volume, then they will see right through any effort to hide the true level of market demand. If the production process is transparent to all firms, then incumbents cannot mislead entrants about their efficiency. And there is no inherent reason why an entrant cannot merely announce *its own intentions to fight tooth and nail*. If saber rattling by the incumbent is more potent than saber rattling by the entrant, it must be due to something besides mere incumbency.

Given the need for asymmetries, we conclude that limit pricing will be much more effective for diversified firms. One reason is that it is much more difficult for rivals to discern their costs. Another is that diversified firms will benefit from establishing a *reputation for toughness*. That is, if they fight hard to protect one market, entrants will be less prone to enter others. Thus, we should expect diversified firms that limit price to defend their turf if entry occurs. To do otherwise would invite further entry into its other markets. Finally, limit pricing can be especially important to diversified firms that sell compatible products. (We discuss product compatibility at much greater length later.) By maintaining a stranglehold on one market, a firm can boost its own sales in the compatible product market.

One of the best documented examples of limit pricing occurred in the early history of xerography. Xerox introduced the world's first plain paper copier in 1960. Xerox held patents on the technology, but a competing technology was available, albeit at a slightly higher cost. Xerox dominated the market but set a price that was apparently well below the monopoly level. According to published research, this limit price reduced the number of entrants by more than half.[5] Limit pricing worked because of critical asymmetries; entrants had little knowledge of market demand and no knowledge of the true costs of Xerox's technology.

It is difficult to conclusively document limit pricing without detailed documents about costs and demand, the exact information that must be hard to get if limit pricing is to be effective. Even so, we can conjecture about which dominant firms currently engage in limit pricing. For example, it seems likely that Microsoft has engaged in limit pricing of its operating system software. One way to do this is to hold down the price of the Windows OS, assuring that Windows remains the operating system of choice on more than 95 percent of personal computers. Microsoft assures that consumers enjoy the bulk of B–C in the short run, but it also assures itself of not having to split P–C with any competitors, for now and the foreseeable future.

The bottom line on limit pricing:

- Take lower profit margins, but enjoy larger market share.
- Low price must convince rivals to stay out.
- There must be asymmetries: in knowledge about market demand, costs, or reputation.

Predatory Pricing

They say in football that the best defense is a good offense. (We wouldn't know about that in Chicago.) The same might be said for firms clinging to their dominant market position. If attacked by a newcomer intent on stealing its business, the best way for an incumbent to respond may be to fight back, slash prices, and drive the upstart out of business. Not only will the incumbent reestablish its monopoly, it will scare off future entrants.

There are lots of examples of predatory pricing. Philip Morris launched the 1993 tobacco price war in the United States for exactly this reason, and it did the same a decade later in South Africa. The breakfast cereal wars drove out some of the off-priced brands, and limited some of the damage caused when new distribution channels opened. When foreign companies set low prices for export goods, competitors in the importing nation call it dumping.

Predators should slash prices with great caution because predatory pricing may violate antitrust laws. Wal-Mart lost a predatory pricing antitrust suit in Arkansas, when three pharmacies argued that Wal-Mart set excessively low prices so as to drive them from the market. Firms must be able to argue that their low prices were reasonable and not designed merely to drive out rivals. Setting prices below variable costs will surely raise red flags with antitrust enforcers, as there is no legitimate economic justification for such low prices other than predation.[6] But incumbents are usually safe from litigation if prices exceed variable costs (Wal-Mart's court defeat in Arkansas was the exception, not the rule). This makes it possible for incumbents to drive less efficient rivals from the market without fear of litigation.

Even so, incumbents should not be too quick to prey on entrants. Predation can harm the incumbents more than entrants. After all, the incumbent is incurring price reductions on a much larger volume of business. Each day that the price war persists, the incumbent will feel more and more as if it is cutting off its nose to spite its face. The principle of asymmetry is at work here, but in reverse. If anything, the incumbent may be more reluctant than the entrant to engage in a price war. And there is no particular reason why the entrant could not start the price war and try to drive the incumbent from the market!

So why do price wars scare away potential entrants? A deep-pocketed incumbent might be able to outlast the entrant. Entrants that lack the wherewithal to ride out a long price war may stay out. Likewise, a low amount of debt on an incumbent's balance sheet might signal to potential entrants the incumbent's ability to handle a price war. (Of course, a deep-pocketed entrant might stay in and choose to ride out the price war. Always look for asymmetries!) If the entrant is uncertain about the incumbent's costs, then it may wonder if predatory pricing is really taking its toll on the incumbent. Each day of additional price cutting reinforces the possibility that the incumbent is still prospering, leaving no hope for the entrant. As with limit pricing, it pays for the incumbent to operate in multiple markets. Diversified firms have more to gain from a reputation for toughness, and smart entrants should understand this (and stay out).

Along these lines, diversified firms may want to aggressively promote toughness by rewarding product managers who vigorously defend market share against new entrants. By rewarding share, rather than profits, individual managers take actions that enhance the entire company's reputation, and translate into higher profits (through entry deterrence) in other markets. Firms should use this strategy sparingly; unless the firm is actively deterring entry, aggressive market share growth will generate short-term losses with possibly no long-term benefits.

The bottom line on predatory pricing:

- Low-cost incumbents can drive out rivals and scare off potential entrants.
- Don't "cut off your nose" to defeat just one entrant; make sure you send a strong signal to other potential entrants.
- Establish that reputation for toughness, especially if you are a diversified firm facing entry in many potential markets.

Excess Capacity

Many firms carry excess capacity. When firms do hold excess capacity, it is usually because they expect an uptick in demand (or have recently experienced an unexpected decline in demand). But when entrants see that incumbents have excess capacity, they may reconsider the prospects for postentry competition, fearing that their entry may trigger an expansion of industry output and a substantial decline in price. The result may be blockaded entry.

Unlike predatory pricing and limit pricing, excess capacity may deter entry even when the entrant possesses complete information about demand, costs, and the incumbent's intentions. The capacity itself serves as the required asymmetry. A monopolist incumbent may leave the idle capacity to serve as a credible commitment that the incumbent will expand output (and depress prices), should entry occur.

Excess capacity is costly and should be used sparingly to deter entry. Here is when it makes sense to carry excess capacity:[7]

- The incumbent has a sustainable cost advantage. This gives it an advantage in the event of entry and a subsequent price war.
- Market demand growth is slow. Otherwise, demand will quickly outstrip capacity.
- The investment in excess capacity must be sunk prior to entry. Otherwise, the entrant might force the incumbent to back off in the event of a price war.
- The potential entrant should not itself be attempting to establish a reputation for toughness.

JUDO ECONOMICS

The conventional wisdom is that when it comes to interfirm rivalry, larger firms have the upper hand. But sometimes, smaller firms and potential entrants can use the incumbent's size to their own advantage. This is known as "judo economics."[8] We have already mentioned how larger firms have more to lose when industry prices fall. This is a powerful deterrent to predatory pricing. If an entrant can convince the incumbent that it does not pose a significant long-term threat to the incumbent's profitability, the incumbent might think twice about incurring large losses to drive the entrant from the market.

Restaurateur and doll company owner Jeffrey Chodorow and real estate developer Arthur Cohen must have had this in mind when they purchased struggling Braniff Airlines in 1988. Braniff went bankrupt the next year. In settling the Braniff assets, Chodorow and Cohen bought the rights to the Braniff trademark for $313,000, took over bankrupt Emerald Airlines, and combined the two into a new Braniff. Braniff publicly announced in the spring of 1991 that it intended to fly out of American Airlines' home city of Dallas, but limit flights to just Los Angeles, New York, Florida, and the Caribbean. By announcing its intention to stay small, Braniff surely hoped that American would not bother to launch a price war.

Braniff started flying scheduled trips in June 1991. It had some immediate setbacks, including flying a banned Boeing 727 into Los Angeles International Airport (the plane violated local noise pollution ordinances). But Braniff's fate was sealed even before its first scheduled flight took off. In a move that many believe was prompted by Braniff's reentry, American Airlines introduced "value pricing" on May 27, 1991, triggering a price war that drove Braniff from the market for good two months later.

If it had stayed true to its word, Braniff would have carried only 3 percent as many passengers as American. So why did American respond aggressively to Braniff's entry? The most likely explanation is that American feared entry by other carriers in Dallas and other markets it served. Thus, American launched a predatory price war not so much to defeat Braniff but to deter entry by others. (The Department of Justice filed predatory pricing charges against American in conjuction with similar pricing tactics in the 1990s, but lost the case because it could not prove that American was losing money as a result of the predatory practices.)

A more successful example of judo economics is provided by Amazon's entry into the online book retail market. Many observers wondered why Barnes & Noble did not immediately respond by establishing their own web site, potentially driving Amazon from the market. Amazon's patented technology was partly to blame, though this raises the question of why Barnes & Noble did not purchase the technology from them. (At the time, Barnes & Noble could have paid more than it was expected to be worth to Amazon.) Perhaps more importantly, Barnes & Noble was reluctant to enter the online market because it feared it would help establish this new market and cannibalize its dominant position in the bricks-and-mortar market. Amazon succeeded beyond the expectations of most market analysts, legitimizing online retailing without any help from Barnes & Noble. Barnes & Noble entered late with an inferior web site, and now lags far behind Amazon in online sales. Even so, total book sales at Barnes & Noble (including bricks-and-mortar stores) are still well ahead of Amazon, and it is difficult to say that Barnes & Noble chose the wrong course.

Netscape's announcement in January 1998 that it would make the source code of its new browser, Communicator 5.0, freely available on the Internet provides yet another example of judo economics. This move enabled sophisticated programmers to customize the Communicator browser to their own idiosyncratic needs. Many firms would be expected to prefer such a customized product to Microsoft's Internet Explorer. Given that Microsoft seemed on the verge of dominating the browser market, why would Microsoft not limit the impact of Netscape's move by permitting customization of its own Internet Explorer browser? Microsoft would be unlikely to do this because its success had been driven by uniformity: All users of Internet Explorer have identical software (just as all users of Microsoft operating systems have identical software). Though Netscape's judo strategy was successful for a while, Microsoft eventually used its clout with PC makers and retailers to establish Internet Explorer as the dominant web browser.

When is it smart to try judo against a larger firm?

- You will take a small share from the incumbent.
- The incumbent must cannibalize a large volume of its own business to retaliate.
- The incumbent is not widely diversified and eager to send a message to other potential entrants.

WRAPPING UP: AN ENTRY DETERRENCE CHECKLIST

All strategic plans must contemplate entry. If entry is not blockaded or accommodated, firms must figure out the best way to deter it. Table 7.1 summarizes the variety of entry barriers discussed in this chapter and the circumstances that make them most effective.

APPENDIX: ENTRY AND THE REAL OPTIONS THEORY OF INVESTMENT

Every business student should be familiar with net present value (NPV) analysis of investments. Entry decisions are very much like investments; they require spending today in the hope of profits in the future. When analyzing an entry opportunity, the analyst computes the discounted NPV of postentry profits and the sunk costs of entry. The difference represents the present value of entry, and a typical decision rule is to enter if the present value is positive. As it turns out, this simple decision rule is wrong. The reason why has spawned a powerful new tool for modeling not only entry decisions, but all major business investment decisions. This tool is derived from the financial analysis of real options and has found broad applications in business strategy. Thus, it is worth exploring the *real options theory of investing*.

Real options theory can involve complex mathematics that we do not present. But the underlying intuition is simple and often sufficient to point analysts in the right direction. Suppose that your firm is considering entering a market. Entry requires $5,000 in sunk investments, such as obtaining regulatory approval or up-front marketing expenses. The payoff for the project is uncertain, so you must compute the *expected net present value* of the investment, which equals the discounted postentry profits minus the $5,000 investment. Let NPV represent the expected net present value. The traditional decision rule is "Invest if NPV > 0." This traditional rule is incorrect. (In an analogous fashion "Do not invest if NPV < 0" is also incorrect. We detail only the first case.)

Table 7.1
Entry Deterrence Checklist

Entry Barrier	Most Effective When	Comment
Sunk costs	Incumbent has incurred them and entrant has not.	Costs must truly be sunk. If incumbent can sell its fixed assets, then so, too, could an entrant. This implies that failure is not very costly, and entry is harder to deter.
Production barriers	Economies of scale or scope, superior access to critical inputs or superior location, process or product patents, or government subsidies.	Must be asymmetric. Technological innovation can lift barriers. Patents are not all equally defensible, and the cost of defending a patent can be prohibitive.
Reputation	Incumbents have longstanding relationships with suppliers and customers.	Reputation reflects hard to measure factors, such as quality or reliability, that entrants may not be able to promise.
Switching costs	There are few supply side barriers to entry.	Can the firm prevent imitation? Do consumers really perceive entrants as different from incumbents?
Tie up access	Channels are few and hard to replicate.	Must share spoils with channel. May arouse antitrust scrutiny.
Limit pricing	Entrants are unsure about demand and/or costs.	May require permanent reduction in profit margins to sustain entry deterrence.
Predatory pricing	Firm has reputation for toughness or competes in multiple markets.	Incumbent firm may lose more than entrant; deep pockets and conviction that there are many potential entrants are a must. May arouse antitrust scrutiny.
Holding excess capacity	Marginal costs are low and flooding the market causes price reductions.	Capacity investments must be sunk. Demand must not be growing.

The problem with this decision rule is that delaying investment helps to resolve uncertainty, and this has value that the decision rule does not take into account. For example, suppose that NPV for this project is $500. You might be tempted to make the investment; after all, it has a positive net present value. But suppose that if you delay investment, you might learn about market demand, supply costs, or competitor intentions. In any event, this news will cause you to update your NPV computation. It might make sense for you to defer your investment until this news is revealed.

Continuing the example, suppose that by delaying the investment a short time, there is a 50 percent chance that you will receive good news: The NPV increases by $2,000, to $2,500. Half the time, you obtain bad news: The NPV decreases by $2,000, to −$1,500. If you obtain the bad news, you would not make the investment, so your actual NPV in this event is $0. Thus, waiting gives you an expected NPV of $1,250: There is a 50 percent chance of $2,500 and a 50 percent chance of $0. This exceeds the NPV of $500 that would be realized if the firm made the investment prior to hearing the news. Thus, unless the firm has a very high discount rate, it pays to wait.

NPV analysis (often enhanced by use of decision trees) is an important first step to analyzing entry and other investment decisions under uncertainty. Often, a sophisticated analysis along these lines is sufficient to capture all of the essential aspects of uncertainty. Sometimes, however, the decision branches become too numerous, especially if uncertainty is resolved slowly over time. When this happens, the analysis must be compromised by unsatisfying assumptions. Fortunately, financial economists have recognized that investment decisions are analogous to decisions to exercise call options and have borrowed methods from the latter to analyze the former.

The analogy is as follows. A call option allows you to buy a share of stock at a particular point in time of your choosing. Once you exercise the call option, you cannot change your mind and exercise it again in the future. Similarly, you can make a business investment at a time of your choosing. But if part of the investment is sunk, then once you make it, there is no turning back. You cannot start from scratch at some future date.

Fischer Black and Myron Scholes derived the formula used to determine the price at which to strike a call option. (Scholes and Robert Merton later received a Nobel Prize in economics for their work on the formula.) The Black–Scholes model is the starting point for the real options theory. Applications of Black–Scholes to business investments are often quite complex. Interested readers can refer to the classic work of Avanish Dixit and Robert Pindyck, *Investment under Uncertainty*, for the mathematical details.[9] In it, Dixit and Pindyck present numerous examples in which firms used the wrong NPVs for decision making and demonstrate that hurdle rates for investments (including entry decisions) are usually much higher than rates used in traditional NPV analysis.

Real options analysis tools are slowly gaining in acceptance as more consulting firms develop the necessary expertise. Many firms have proprietary software that greatly simplifies the analytic tasks. Some major corporations have developed their own in-house capabilities to perform real options analysis. One of the first was pharmaceutical giant Merck, which began using real options theory as early as 1994 under the guidance of chief financial officer Judy Lewent. Today, Merck and other leading pharmaceutical companies use real options to plan billions of dollars in investments in dozens of R&D projects. Real options models have been adapted to many other industrial settings, including petroleum drilling and investment in fisheries. Like pharmaceutical R&D, these industries must make substantial sunk investments under considerable uncertainty.

NOTES

1. T. Dunne, M. J. Roberts, and L. Samuelson, "Patterns of Firm Entry and Exit in U.S. Manufacturing Industries," *RAND Journal of Economics* (Winter 1988): pp. 495–515.

2. A lessee must usually commit to 24 months, or $1.2 million per plane. But lessees can often sublease their planes if they want to exit the market. Thus, aircraft costs should not be a major deterrent to entering the airline business.

3. This is taken from Joseph Bain's discussion in *Barriers to New Competition: Their Character and Consequences in Manufacturing Industries*, Cambridge, MA: Harvard University Press, 1956, and C. C. Von Weizsäcker in *Barriers to Entry: A Theoretical Treatment*, Berlin: Springer-Verlag, 1980.

4. R. Smiley, "Empirical Evidence on Strategic Entry Deterrence," *International Journal of Industrial Organization* 6 (1988): pp. 167–180.

5. E. Blackstone, "Limit Pricing in the Copying Machine Industry," *Quarterly Review of Economics and Business* 12 (1972): pp. 57–65.

6. For a more thorough discussion of relevant issues, see A. Edlin and J. Farrell, "The American Airlines Case: A Chance to Clarify Predation Policy" in *The Antitrust Revolution*, edited by J. Kwoka and L. White, New York: Oxford University Press, 2004.

7. For more details, see Marvin B. Lieberman, "Strategies for Capacity Expansion," *Sloan Management Review* (Summer 1987): pp. 19–25.

8. J. Gelman and S. Salop, "Judo Economics: Capacity Limitation and Coupon Competition," *Bell Journal of Economics* 14 (1983): pp. 315–325.

9. A. K. Dixit and R. S. Pindyck, *Investment under Uncertainty*, Princeton, NJ: Princeton University Press, 1994.

CHAPTER 8

HOW TO SUSTAIN YOUR COMPETITIVE ADVANTAGE

To be successfully positioned, your firm must offer a value proposition—a level of B–C—that surpasses what your rivals can offer. To do this, your firm must possess scarce and immobile resources and capabilities. If these are scopable, so much the better. Possessing scarce, immobile, and scopable resources and capabilities may be necessary for success, but it is not sufficient, because competition and entry pose persistent threats. If competitors and entrants are sufficiently differentiated or fail to offer the same B–C, then there is little to fear. But sometimes rivals can develop their own stocks of resources and capabilities that duplicate your value creation proposition. This would effectively neutralize the source of your firm's competitive advantage. Your market share may plummet, price competition may intensify, and profits may disappear.

The manager of any successful firm must constantly worry about whether other firms can mimic its success in delivering value. What is especially nettlesome is that rivals do not have to make an exact copy of the business model, but need only copy the value creation proposition. For example, Xerox's advantage in the plain paper copier market in the 1970s was built, in part, on superior servicing capabilities backed by a network of dealers who provided on-site service calls. Canon successfully challenged Xerox in the small copier market by building highly reliable machines that rarely broke down and did not have to be serviced as often as Xerox's. Canon's superior product neutralized Xerox's

177

advantage by diminishing the value of its servicing capabilities and its dealer network. To take another example, Sears enjoyed a decades-long advantage in the appliance retailing market, thanks largely to the goodwill of its brand name. When the marketing revolution enabled companies like Maytag and Whirlpool to establish their own brand reputations, it paved the way for retailers such as Circuit City and Wal-Mart to compete on the basis of distribution expertise without having to match Sears's brand caché.

The factors that protect incumbents from mimicry are called *isolating mechanisms*. These are to a firm what an entry barrier is to an industry. Just as an entry barrier impedes new entrants from coming into an industry and competing away profits from incumbent firms, isolating mechanisms prevent other firms—existing competitors and entrants alike—from competing away the extra profit that a firm earns from its competitive advantage. Perhaps the most critical strategic challenge of the manager of a successful firm is to assess, establish, and maintain the firm's isolating mechanisms.

There are two main groups of isolating mechanisms:

1. *Impediments to imitation:* These impede existing firms and potential entrants from duplicating the resources and capabilities that form the basis of the firm's advantage. For example, many firms compete in the golf club market, but few have been able to match Callaway's distinctive capabilities in designing innovative clubs and bringing them quickly to market.

2. *Early-mover advantages:* Once a firm acquires a competitive advantage, these isolating mechanisms increase the economic power of that advantage over time, making it more difficult to match the firm's ability to create value for its customers. Cisco Systems, for example, dominates the market for products such as routers and switches, which link together local area networks (LANs). Its success in this business has helped establish its Cisco Internetwork Operating System (Cisco IOS) software as an industry standard. This, in turn, has a feedback effect that benefits Cisco's entire line of networking products.

IMPEDIMENTS TO IMITATION

Some impediments to imitation are easy to describe, if challenging to put in place. Legal restrictions, such as patents, copyrights, and trademarks, give incumbent firms obvious advantages. In fact, patent-protected products, such as prescription drugs, routinely provide higher returns on investments than any other group of products. Government control over entry into markets, through licensing, certification, or quotas on operating rights, can also be powerful impediments to imitation.

Firms can buy patents, copyrights, trademarks, and operating rights, seemingly establishing a competitive advantage overnight. Drug companies purchase the rights to distribute the discoveries of small biotech firms, television networks buy rights to broadcast sports events, and big software makers buy the product catalogs of smaller rivals. None of these strategies create a sustainable competitive advantage, however, because the buyers are acquiring mobile assets and must pay competitive prices to get them. The only exception is if the buyer can deploy the asset in ways that other prospective purchasers cannot, and therefore can acquire the asset at a discount relative to its value (the price being determined by the value the asset delivers to other purchasers). This is not generally true for biotech products, sports events, or computer software, and while these acquisitions may help big firms get bigger, they do not usually help them earn economic profits.

This is not to say that you can never prosper by acquiring scarce, valuable assets. To do so, *you must obtain them on terms that your rivals cannot replicate.* At one time, Topps monopolized the market for baseball cards in the United States by signing every professional baseball player to a long-term contract, giving Topps the exclusive right to market the player's picture on baseball cards sold with gum or candy. Although the players were mobile assets free to sell marketing rights to anyone, they sold their rights one player at a time, increasing the appeal of selling to Topps while diluting their individual bargaining power. The result was that Topps dominated the market, earned handsome profits, and faced no rivals. Had the players been organized through a union, they could have secured a far higher percentage of the profits. Nowadays, the major league baseball (MLB) players' union negotiates highly lucrative rights deals for trading cards, uniforms, and other paraphernalia, and Topps faces stiff competition from Bowman and Upper Deck.

The flip side of superior access to inputs is superior access to customers. A firm that secures access to the best distribution channels or the most productive retail locations will outcompete its rivals for customers. Like Topps and the baseball players, this strategy works best when the firm can secure individual distributors/retailers one by one. Edward Jones (EJ) is a full-service brokerage firm and as such, competes with other full-service firms, such as Merrill Lynch, Salomon Smith Barney, Morgan Stanley Dean Witter, Prudential Securities, and PaineWebber. Edward Jones, often called the Wal-Mart of Wall Street, has built a distribution system for selling financial services to a customer segment that is difficult to reach due to geographic distance and/or their lower propensity for seeking out financial services. Typical clients include small business owners, farmers and teachers who are saving and investing for retirement, and retirees who want to generate income and preserve their assets. In fact, there is much about this segment that makes them ideal clients for these services: (1) There are so many of them and (2), they do not churn their accounts. Edward Jones can use this feature of their clients to obtain better terms from, for example, their mutual fund suppliers.

While these customers were under the radar of EJ's competitors, EJ has essentially locked up this desirable segment with its astounding 8,500 offices in the United States, plus hundreds more in Canada and the United Kingdom.

There are three basic takeaways from this discussion:

1. Acquiring scarce assets does not by itself assure success.
2. Acquiring cospecialized assets can assure success, as rivals will be unable to create the same value and will be unwilling to outbid you for them.
3. Acquire a network of cospecialized assets; the whole will be greater than the sum of the parts, and again your rivals will be unwilling to outbid you.

Intangible Barriers to Imitation

Sometimes, it is difficult to pin down the reasons for a firm's success. This is not such a bad thing, because it makes it difficult for others to copy it. Business scholars have created a cottage industry out of studying Wal-Mart's distribution systems, yet no one has been able to completely match them. Wal-Mart's capabilities were developed through years of patient trial and error refined through practice and experience, and cannot be articulated as an algorithm, formula, or set of rules. Much of the know-how and collective wisdom inside any organization is of this sort and is rarely written down or codified in procedures manuals. As a result, even the firm's managers may be unable to describe persuasively what they do better than their rivals. While this is a powerful impediment to imitation by other firms, it may also limit the ability of firms to grow beyond their traditional business lines. (By the same token, it can lead to complacency, as average firms convince themselves that they have intangible advantages; this reaffirms the need to document value creation through careful measurement, as described in Chapter 4.)

Another hard-to-pin-down source of sustainable advantage are those capabilities that arise from socially complex managerial processes. These include the interpersonal relations of managers in a firm and the relationship between the firm's managers and those of its suppliers and customers. Every one of Toyota's competitors may understand that an important contributor to Toyota's success is the trust that exists between it and its component suppliers. But it is difficult to create such trust, however desirable it may be.

If the sources of sustained competitive advantage are often complex and difficult to articulate, they will also be hard to consciously redesign. This is one reason why so many complex mergers may look good on paper but fail utterly in practice. If only AOL, Daimler Benz, and Disney had taken greater care to identify the sources of competitive advantage in their target companies before they embarked on some of the most ill-advised acquisitions of recent years (of Time-Warner, Chrysler, and Cap Cities/ABC, respectively). Not only was it hard for the acquirers to find promised synergies, they managed to destroy much of the value in their targets by attempting to remake them in their own images. Time-Warner was not ready to become a bastion of entrepreneurs; Chrysler was not ready to change target markets; Cap Cities/ABC was unprepared for centralized decision making on key issues such as program scheduling, and ABC head programming guru Jamie Tarses resigned over the resulting conflicts.[1]

Strategic Fit

Firms represent collections of complex practices. Ideally, these practices should complement each other, making each more effective. Paul Milgrom and John Roberts coined the term *complementarities* to describe synergies among organizational practices.[2] We introduced the concept of complementarities in Chapter 3, in conjunction with the discussion of strategic fit. Complementarity business practices can be a powerful impediment to imitation and are worth another look.

Recall how Southwest Airlines has achieved strategic fit in its numerous business practices. Southwest strives for the fastest turnaround of any airline, often landing a plane and departing in less than half the time of other carriers. To do this, Southwest chooses (or more accurately avoids) particular activities. Southwest does not serve meals or assign seats, uses a single type of plane, and avoids flying into congested airports. Taken together, these strategies help Southwest avoid the kinds of bottlenecks that sometimes cripple rival carriers.

Harvard's Michael Porter has forcefully argued that strategic fit among processes is essential to firms seeking a long-term competitive advantage over their rivals. Not only does each process make the others more effective, but it is difficult for other firms to copy the strategy. Firms that have pursued an entirely different set of processes could not just copy one at a time. They would have to copy them all at once, and this could be quite a difficult undertaking.

For many firms struggling to get ahead, the problem is not enumerating the business practices of their successful rivals. United Airlines can easily identify Southwest's business practices: Use a single type of plane, emphasize point-to-point travel, no onboard catering, and so on. The problem is trying to emulate these practices. United is committed to its hub at Chicago's O'Hare Airport and to serving mainly hub-and-spoke passengers. Unless it moves out of O'Hare and focuses on point-to-point traffic, United cannot hope to match Southwest's operational efficiencies. Converting to a single type of aircraft, or eliminating on-board catering, is hardly feasible given the length of many of United's hauls, and would do little to improve service to the level enjoyed by Southwest. This is not United's fault; it has pursued a market segment—hub-and-spoke traffic— that does not offer the same opportunities for complementarities.

Even when there is no single barrier to imitation, the imperative of emulating successfully each and every practice can be daunting, as a bit of mathematics demonstrates. Suppose a firm has successfully meshed 10 related practices. Suppose also that a rival can identify all 10 and has a reasonably high probability of implementing any one of them successfully, say 80 percent. The chances of the rival implementing all 10 practices successfully is $.80^{10} = .11$, or 11 percent. In this way, the mathematics of probabilities serves as a powerful impediment to imitation.

THE EARLY MOVER ADVANTAGE

Confederate Civil War General Nathan Bedford Forrest was famous for leading his cavalry soldiers into battle with the directive to "get there firstest with the mostest." Many managers are under pressure to be the "firstest with the mostest" in their product markets. This is especially true in the technology sector, about which one analyst stated, "First-mover advantage has become religion in the industry."[3] If there really is a first-mover advantage in a market, then the first firm in will enjoy a powerful isolating mechanism and a better than average chance of sustaining success.

Unfortunately, the analytic tools that we have presented thus far do not make much of a case either for or against early movers. We firmly believe that success goes to those firms that create the most B–C while avoiding competition and entry. There is no prima facie case that being first has anything to do with creating or protecting B–C. In fact, there are many good examples of successful late movers. One need only look at technology markets, where being first has almost religious significance, to become an unbeliever. Atari was the first serious entrant into the video game market, but was wiped out when Nintendo launched its Nintendo Entertainment System in 1983. IBM introduced the first personal computers, but

Compaq became the first successful home PC brand, and Dell eventually supplanted them both. Even a frequently mentioned first mover, Amazon.com, followed three other booksellers in the online marketplace.

If first-mover advantage is an iffy proposition for technology industries, then it is even less of a sure thing in other industries. By observing their rivals, learning from mistakes, and finding profitable niches, second movers often enjoy greater prosperity than industry guinea pigs. Let's take a closer look at the late movers that we just discussed. By observing Atari's troubled relationships with programmers and retailers alike (who were barely making any profit from Atari's gaming system), Nintendo learned the importance of assuring profits throughout the value chain of video gaming. They wrote contracts with game developers and retailers that assured everyone a share of the profits. The result was higher quality games and a better retail experience (through special World of Nintendo shops). Compaq observed that early PC adopters were very savvy about the components that went inside the box. The Seagate hard drive, the Intel microprocessor, and the Microsoft operating system mattered more than the name on the box. By assembling PCs from reliable components, Compaq overcame any brand awareness that may have served IBM well in the mainframe market but was relatively worthless for PCs. Michael Dell observed that all the traditional PC makers suffered massive inventory losses due to technological obsolescence, and devised a made-to-order production process that minimized inventory holdings. Amazon learned from other firms' early forays into online retailing that consumers valued streamline search-and-order fulfillment as much or more than low prices.

True believers in the first-mover advantage must reconcile themselves with a basic business fact. First movers often fail. Call it the *testing the waters* argument. First movers are prone to make mistakes that can be difficult to undo. Whenever there is great uncertainty about the appropriate business model, moving later has its advantages.

IN DEFENSE OF EARLY MOVERS

This is not to say that moving second is always superior to moving first. When conditions are right, early movers can establish isolating mechanisms that protect them, even when rivals learn their secrets and improve upon them. Some of the factors that favor early movers are the importance of seller reputation, learning economies, and switching costs.

Seller Reputation and Buyer Uncertainty

Recall from Chapter 6 that consumers often rely on personal experience when purchasing products for which quality is important. As a result, early entrants in the market for experience goods may enjoy an advantage. If consumers are unsure about the quality of competing products, they will usually stick with whatever has worked well in the past. The brand name of a high quality incumbent can thus become a powerful isolating mechanism. Once the firm's reputation is established, it will have an advantage competing for new customers. With an ever growing base of satisfied customers, its advantage will grow. Lesser-known brands become marginalized and forced to fill niches where either reputation does not matter or the incumbent does not serve.

IBM's competitive advantage in the market for mainframes was, for years, sustained by considerations such as these. The famous old saying, "You'll never get fired for buying an IBM," captures this point. In the 1970s, one industry expert said that it would take at least a 30 percent difference in the price-performance ratio to induce a customer to choose a competing brand over IBM. The resilience of the Tylenol brand against competitors following its 1984 tampering crisis is another good example of the advantage that pioneering brands can enjoy.

The Learning Curve

From airframe manufacturing to open heart surgery, from playing video games to playing the flute, experience and effectiveness go hand in hand. The results are tangible: lower manufacturing costs and better patient outcomes, record high game scores and beautiful music. These examples are just the tip of the iceberg; hundreds of studies confirm that there is a learning curve in seemingly every human endeavor. A large body of research finds that doubling cumulative production experience leads to 10 percent to 30 percent lower production costs. Research shows that learning boosts quality as well.

When a firm faces a learning curve, production today generates savings in the future. An important implication is that the true economic cost of current production is less than the current accounting cost, due to the offsetting reduction in future costs. Though accountants may balk at thinking about costs this way, firms that fail to do so may miss out on opportunities to boost profits. Firms facing a steep learning curve should ramp up production in the short run, even to the point of posting short-term accounting losses. These firms will enjoy lower production costs in the future, and assuming demand is somewhat predictable, these are savings the firm can bank on. There is also a strategic benefit to moving down the learning curve, as this will make the firm a more formidable competitor when faced with future entry.

Learning is especially important for goods and services for which complex tasks are performed repeatedly, such as surgery. Many research studies document a powerful learning curve for medical procedures. The result is that more experienced providers produce better outcomes at lower costs. We see the evidence of this in many geographic markets, where there is often just one hospital that performs the lion's share of difficult procedures such as liver transplants or cochlear implants. Combining an understanding of the learning curve with a lack of faith in markets, health care regulators in many nations (and in some states in the United States) limit the number of providers allowed to perform complex procedures.

The Boston Consulting Group Growth/Share Paradigm

Beginning in the 1970s, the Boston Consulting Group (BCG) made aggressive pursuit of learning the foundation for corporate strategy when it introduced the *growth/share matrix*. Figure 8.1 depicts a typical BCG matrix. The matrix distinguishes products on two dimensions: growth of the market in which the product is situated, and the product's market

Figure 8.1
The BCG Growth/Share Matrix

The growth/share matrix divides products into four categories according to their potential for growth and relative market share. Some strategists recommended that firms use the profits earned from cash cows to ramp up production of rising stars and problem children. As the latter products move down their learning curves, they become cash cows in the next investment cycle.

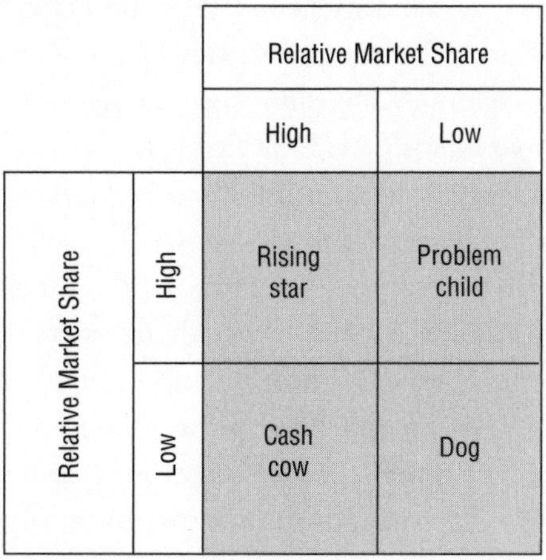

		Relative Market Share	
		High	Low
Relative Market Share — High		Rising star	Problem child
Relative Market Share — Low		Cash cow	Dog

share relative to the share of its next largest competitors. A product line is classified into one of four categories:

1. A *rising star* is a product in a growing market with a high relative share.
2. A *cash cow* is a product in a stable or declining market with a high relative share.
3. A *problem child* is a product in a growing market with a low relative share.
4. A *dog* is a product in a stable or declining market with a low relative share.

The original BCG strategy for successfully managing a portfolio of products is based on taking advantage of learning curves and the product life cycle. BCG felt that its clients should increase production in the early stages of the product's life cycle to secure learning economies. Firms could use profits from cash cow products to fund increased production of problem child and rising star products. Learning economies

would cement the advantages of rising stars while enabling some problem children to become more competitive. As their markets matured
and demand slackened, these products would then become cash cows to
support learning strategies in new emerging markets.

Though appealing on the surface, the growth-share paradigm has
two major flaws. The first is the sole reliance on internal capital markets
to fund new ventures. Venture capitalists are more than willing to spon-
sor aggressive growth by startups; witness the meteoric rises (and sometimes catastrophic crashes) of biotech companies like Genzyme and
Occulon. Thus, the paradigm offers no unique benefits as a basis for
corporate strategy; it is easily mimicked by independent firms.

The second flaw in the growth-share matrix arises from the overly
broad application of the learning strategy. Though critical to the success
of many organizations, experience is no panacea, as we now discuss.

When Does a Learning Strategy Make Sense?

Before aggressively increasing output in quest of a learning advantage,
managers must answer several questions about the tasks to be learned
and the marketplace for the products:

1. *How steep is the learning curve?* Some tasks are easily mastered, giving little advantage to early movers. Even complex tasks may provide little deterrence to newcomers, provided they can outsource
   them. The retailing of prescription drugs provides a nice case in
   point. Although established pharmacies like Walgreen's and
   RiteAid have dominated the market for decades, a lack of experience did not seem to matter to mail-order pharmacies like Medco
   and Express Scripts. Begun only about 20 years ago, these upstarts
   quickly carved a niche in the market, garnering double digit
   shares of the market for chronic drugs.

   Mail-order pharmacies were scarcely at a learning disadvantage
   relative to the bricks-and-mortar giants, despite the many complexities involved in retailing drugs. All pharmacies rely on independent regional warehouses for distribution expertise; mail-order
   pharmacies simply tapped into existing warehouses. The drug

makers themselves helped develop software to enable the new-comers to track sales and monitor patient compliance. The mail-order pharmacies may have lacked the personal relationships with patients that take years to develop, but this did not matter to patients with chronic illnesses who refill the same prescriptions without need for consultation.

2. *Is learning firm-specific or task-specific?* If learning is firm–specific, then skilled workers lose mobility and the firm can capture the value that its experienced workers create. On the other hand, if learning is task-specific, then skilled workers can shop around their talents and capture the value for themselves in the form of higher wages. The distinction between firm– and task-specific learning is closely related to the concept of cospecialized assets. Both arise when workers develop their skills in a team atmosphere, where interactions of key personnel are critical to overall success. Firms always prefer their assets to be cospecialized and learning to be firm–specific.

   Managers must usually rely on their judgment to determine if learning is firm– or task-specific. But thanks to extensive data from the Medicare program, health services researchers are producing mounting evidence that surgery displays firm-specific learning. Experienced surgeons have better surgical outcomes, but only when they treat patients at the hospital where they perform most of their procedures. The benefits of experience virtually disappear when surgeons treat patients elsewhere. Health services researchers surmise that the surgeon's skill is tied to the experience of the entire surgical team.

3. *How stable is the technology and market demand?* Recall the discussion of Disney's resources and capabilities in Chapter 3. The success of Disney's animated motion picture division was predicated on more than just the brilliance of Jeffrey Katzenberg. Disney studio animators had decades of experience that no other studio could rival. The release of Pixar Studio's *Toy Story* destroyed much of the value of Disney's experience. Pixar's computer-generated animation made the art of drawing animated cels obsolete, as moviegoers of all ages preferred the dazzling colors and sharper

images that Pixar's programmers brought to the big screen. Today, computer-animated films dominate old-fashioned, hand-drawn animation at the box office. Even Katzenberg's biggest successes at Dreamworks—the two *Shrek* movies—were computer-generated.[4]

In addition to answering these questions, the manager must carefully assess whether the answers vary across functional areas of the organization.

Production   Experience helps when the production technology is complex yet evolves incrementally. Think microprocessor chips. Do not think personal computers (which are easily assembled from components).

Marketing and Sales   Experience in sales matters most when products and services are highly customized and it takes time for the selling staff to learn how to match the firm's offering to customer needs. But if rival firms can offer equal levels of customization, then salespeople are mobile and the benefits of experience are lost. Think retailing of made-to-order goods, such as supercomputers or haute couture fashion. Do not think auto insurance (sales agents know about individual customer needs, but even upstart firms can customize features).

Research and Development   Experience matters as long as the underlying science remains grounded in an established paradigm. Experience then conveys an advantage to the firm provided the research team is tied to cospecialized assets owned by that firm. For example, experience matters a lot in discipline-based academic research. But experience is not enough to assure the success of major research universities. When universities hire star scientists, they build them expensive laboratories and, in exchange, impose strict rules about ownership of patents. (To give an idea of the stakes involved in limiting asset mobility, Northwestern University stands to make $100 million or more from one recent patent.)

The analyst can put all of this information together in the learning curve matrix presented in Table 8.1. If learning in a functional area is steep, firm-specific, and stable, the firm has a basis for pursuing a learning curve strategy in that area. If learning is steep and stable, but task-specific rather than firm-specific, the firm must find ways to limit labor mobility before pursuing a learning strategy.

Learning and Organizations

Firms that rely on experience to gain competitive advantage should organize their operations to maximize learning. Encourage workers to share their experiences about what works and what does not. (This was an important function of the famous Japanese work groups of the 1960s and 1970s.) If learning is task-specific, be sure to establish career ladders that are organized around those tasks and encourage experienced workers to share their task-knowledge with younger colleagues. Rotate task assignments (within the department) of hot-shot younger workers to ensure that tomorrow's managers have task-specific knowledge of all the workers they supervise. If knowledge is firm-specific, then feel free to move workers across departments or divisions of the firm, spreading their firm-knowledge with them. With firm-specific learning, it is especially important for senior managers to have experience across the entire organization.

Personnel practices can make or break learning organizations. Nucor is a great example of a firm with incentive programs and personnel practices based on the principle that, under the right conditions, firm

Table 8.1
The Learning Curve Matrix

	Production	R&D	Marketing
Is learning steep?			
Is learning specific to task or to firm?			
Is learning stable?			

learning can be converted into shareholder wealth. The organizational learning at Nucor has led the firm to greater efficiency and thus lower production costs. Employees are grouped into teams in which newer employees are continuously trained by more senior employees, in the process learning multiple functions in the firm. This leads to more productive employees and allows full capacity utilization at all times, as workers can shift to the part of the process requiring the most attention. This practice fits with the incentive program; bonuses are paid on group performance so members of the group have an incentive to train one another. Nucor has historically hired the people who build its plants to work in them. This may promote a certain pride in ownership, and the practice increases the workers' knowledge of the plant's function. Finally, Nucor's compensation policies—profit sharing, stock options, college allowance for employees' children, and so on—reduce turnover. This keeps accumulated experience in the firm and avoids the costly training of new employees.

How did Nucor come up with this set of practices? Put simply, experience. Nucor has extensive experience building and operating steel plants, so its managers have moved down a learning curve, finding the right set of human resources practices to enhance employee learning. And this learning curve, combined with the strategic fit of all these elements, prevents other firms from copying these strategies.

On the downside, Lockheed's personnel practices during the 1980s prevented it from fully exploiting learning opportunities in the production of the L-1011 TriStar.[5] Lockheed's union contract required it to promote experienced line workers to management. This produced a domino effect whereby as many as 10 workers changed jobs when 1 was moved to a management position. As a result, workers were forced to learn tasks that their higher ranking co-workers had already mastered. By moving the most skilled workers up and out, learning was stifled. This and related policies reduced labor productivity at Lockheed by as much as 40 percent to 50 percent annually.

While codifying work rules and reducing job turnover facilitate retention of knowledge, these steps may stifle creativity. Workers learn to do things the old way rather than continually improvise new methods.

Managers must have a deft touch to strike the correct balance between stability and change. Codification of work rules developed through prior experience makes sense when the production technology is stabilizing and the skills of the labor force are diminishing. But it still pays to give highly skilled workers the freedom to try new ideas in more volatile environments.

Switching Costs

Switching costs are another important source of sustainable advantage. When products are virtual commodities, introducing switching costs is an attractive way to soften competition and generate profits. Telecommunications is fundamentally a commodity business, yet AT&T has enjoyed long spells of dominance, first in long distance, and more recently in cellular service. Some of their sustained success can be credited to traditional entry barriers: government regulations, limited bandwidth (which is a variant of limited distribution channels), and high fixed costs. But AT&T has also benefited from substantial consumer switching costs in many of its product lines.

AT&T introduced toll-free 800 dialing in 1967. When other long distance carriers entered the market in the 1970s, they also offered 800 service. But until the early 1990s, businesses that switched from AT&T to Sprint or MCI could not keep their 800 numbers. This made the cost of switching prohibitive, as businesses would have to inform all of their customers about the number change (and, in the case of catchy numbers such as 1-800-FLOWERS, give up a critical asset of the firm). Commercial and residential cellular phone users faced the same problem with their personal phone numbers until 2003, when the Federal Communications Commission finally made cellular phone numbers portable. AT&T dominated both markets for many years, in no small measure due to the resulting customer switching costs. Prices for 800 service and cellular service dropped once those numbers became portable.

Early movers who create switching costs enjoy a twofold advantage. As noted earlier, switching costs soften competition. But even before incumbents face competition, switching costs make it hard for entrants to gain much of a toehold in the market. This makes them a powerful source of first–mover advantage.

NETWORK EFFECTS

Microsoft Windows. Sony Playstation. eBay. These are some of the most successful new products of the past two decades. What they share in common, in addition to being part of the world of hi tech, is the presence of *network effects*. Network effects are one of the most powerful sources of sustained advantage, and the battle to create a dominant network can make or break a firm and even an entire industry.

A product displays network effects or *network externalities* when consumers value the product more if other consumers also use it. In some networks, such as telephone and e-mail networks, consumers are physically linked. The network effect arises because if the network has more users, there are greater opportunities for communication. In other cases, the network effect arises from the use of complementary goods, such as DVD software complementing DVD hardware. As the number of DVD hardware owners increases, the demand for movies goes up. This increases the supply of movies, enhancing the demand for hardware. The reinforcing cycle then repeats.

A prime example of a company that has created a sustainable advantage through network effects is eBay. In 1995 eBay was launched by Pierre Omidyar, who created the Internet site to help his girlfriend buy and sell Pez dispensers. Today, one can buy almost anything at eBay, even expensive jewelry, new homes, and the occasional Ferrari! Buyers like eBay because there are so many items for sale and because there are often several sellers of the same items, even obscurities. In addition, eBay offers buyers information about the credibility of sellers. Sellers like eBay because there are so many buyers. Thus, the sheer volume of transactions on eBay brings buyers and sellers back for more.[6]

Networks and Standards

In the late nineteenth century, the U.S. railroad industry suffered from needless inefficiencies due to incompatible tracking. The rails in one state might be 4 feet 7 inches apart; in a neighboring state, they might be 5 feet apart! Railroad crews had to stop their trains at the state line, unload, and reload onto a new train. (This problem still exists in other parts of the world.) Eventually, the industry coalesced around the Northern Standard gauge of track, with a width of 4 feet, 8.5 inches, and the efficiency of the nation's rail network improved immeasurably. In the modern economy, the list of products and services that depend on standards seems endless: cellular communications, personal computing, the Internet, video gaming, high definition television, and surround sound processing for home theater, just to name a few.

Once a standard is established, it can be very difficult to replace. For example, the QWERTY standard for keyboards emerged in the 1860s and remains dominant, despite having lost its original technological advantage. (The mechanical QWERTY keyboard was less prone to jamming than other keyboard configurations.) Standard-setting is a potentially potent source of sustainable competitive advantage, especially when standards are established for products with network effects. The advantage to a firm from having its technology adapted as the standard can be substantial. The firm enjoys royalties on its technology, may sell complementary goods, and may gain a lead in developing the next generation of products. The world's most valuable company, Microsoft, provides ample evidence of this. MS-DOS may not have been the best PC operating system available in the 1980s (Apple's window-driven system was surely better), but with virtually all software designed to run on MS-DOS machines, and virtually all computer users working with MS-DOS machines and software, the feedback effects of the network proved unstoppable.

In many industries in which standards could exist, we do not necessarily see convergence to a single standard. For example, five years after the introduction of competing high resolution audio formats (Super Audio CD and DVD-Audio), the two continue to share a small market while potential adopters sit on the fence waiting for one or the other to emerge dominant. Failure to adopt a single standard can cripple an industry if there are resulting cost increases. This is especially likely if product is used in conjunction with a complementary good that is costly to produce and/or distribute. This appears to be one factor limiting the success of high resolution audio, where it is costly to master recordings in each format, and retailers lack the space to stock the same title in multiple formats (in addition to stocking traditional compact discs).

COMPETING IN NETWORK MARKETS: IS IT BETTER TO WIN OR TO SHARE?

In markets with network externalities, the first firm or technology to establish a critical mass of customers can dominate, achieving close to 100 percent market share. Managers in these markets understand the need to establish a large base of customers early on. Managers face an additional challenge early in the life of these markets: They must decide whether to compete for the market, by establishing the dominant technology standard, or compete in the market, by sharing the market with other firms using the same standard. Here are five key principles for choosing which route to take.

1. *Don't forget the Value Net.* Rapid growth requires access to critical inputs and distribution channels. Suppliers and distributors must derive some benefit from supporting your product rather than the competition, not just during the early days of the market, but also as they look to the future, after you (or your rival) have established a dominant market position. The electronics companies that supported DVD—mainly Sony, Matsushita, and Toshiba—succeeded to a large extent because they made DVD an open technology without patent protection. This assured suppliers (the movie studios) and distributors (electronics retailers) that there would be ample profits for everyone.

2. *Be sure to appeal to early adopters.* Almost every new technology product follows a predictable pattern. Initially, firms set prices high and sell to early adopters who are willing to pay a steep premium to be the first to try a new product. Prices decline gradually at first, attracting early fence sitters who have been waiting for bugs in the beta versions to be worked out. By the third generation, the product is priced for the mass market. Although sales to

early adopters may amount to no more than 1 percent of total product category sales, the influence of early adopters belies their numbers. They create the industry buzz, provide enormous word of mouth (late adopters often look to the early adopters for advice), and may influence magazine selections for product reviews. Early adopters are especially influential in markets with network externalities; makers of complementary goods will observe which way the market is moving and produce accordingly.

This dynamic was certainly true in the DVD/DIVX war. Early adopters preferred DVD, which offered superior quality (such as remastered video, wide-screen production, and Director's Comments). Early adopters also feared that Circuit City's introduction of the competing DIVX format would confuse the market and limit demand for both formats. Some early adopters were so upset that they visited Circuit City stores and bad-mouthed DIVX in front of potential customers! DIVX sales failed to come close to initial expectations and Circuit City pulled the plug less than a year after product launch. Early adopters were quickly rewarded with a flood of new DVD movies. To this day, some early adopters continue to boycott Circuit City, whose failure to embrace DVD contributed to a decline in market share behind Best Buy from which it has yet to recover.

The firms that made up the DVD consortium faced several difficult choices early on. One was how to build a critical mass for the DVD format. But prior to that, they had to decide whether to work together, effectively competing in the market, or try to establish their own standards, thereby competing for the market. Circuit City chose the latter path and suffered irreparable harm. Twenty years prior, Sony had experienced the same fate when it had launched the Betamax videotape format in direct competition with a consortium-backed VHS technology. Sony seems to have repeated history by launching its Super Audio CD (SACD) high resolution audio format in direct competition with DVD-Audio.

3. *Half a monopoly is better than half a duopoly.* Sometimes, seemingly unpredictable factors help determine the outcome of a standards battle. This was partly the case in the Betamax/VHS battle. The

Beta format was more compact and offered slightly better video and audio quality. The VHS format offered a longer playing time per tape. The hardware competitors were unsure which features would be most embraced by consumers. Had Sony joined the VHS consortium, it would have been guaranteed a share of oligopoly profits. But going it alone offered it a chance for monopoly profits, in the event that consumers favored quality over endurance.

The lure of monopoly profits cannot be dismissed. After all, it is better to be a monopolist half the time than a duopolist all the time.[7] This is especially true if product market competition is very intense. Thus, it was probably worth the risk to Sony to go for the whole market. (As it turned out, the biggest use of VCRs was for playing movies, which favored the longer-playing VHS tapes.)

4. *Avoid competition in the complementary goods markets.* When competitors opt for incompatibility, both may invest heavily in promoting their product, lining up complementary product vendors, and so on, in the belief that whoever invests the most will win the standards war. When such investments seem likely, compatibility (competing in the market) is likely a better choice, lest the firms compete away nearly all of the profits in an effort to establish a dominant market position, as has happened in the market for some consumer electronics.

5. *Avoid prolonged standards battles.* In some markets with network externalities, success depends on the growth of markets for complementary products. Competition between standards setters may keep complementary products markets on the fence, thereby reducing demand for the product category. This has occurred in the high resolution audio market. Most major music labels have adopted a wait and see attitude, preferring to defer production costs until they determine which format, if either, will prevail. Sony has the advantage of owning its own music catalog and released hundreds of SACD titles early on in the standards battle. But Sony has effectively halted release of additional SACDs, even as the penetration of SACD compatible hardware has recently started to grow.

THINGS HAPPEN

There is an old sports adage that "It is better to be lucky than good." Sports fans do not take this too seriously—Michael Jordan did not win six NBA championships through luck—but it does remind us that there is some element of chance in all forms of competition. This is just as true in competitive markets as it is in sports. Sony Music Entertainment once again serves to illustrate the concept.

Sony Entertainment expected big things from the November 18, 2003, release of the Michael Jackson *Number Ones* compact disc. Three years earlier, the Beatles' *One*, another anthology of greatest hits (released by Capitol Records), shot to the top of the charts. Expectations for *Number Ones* were dashed when, on the very day of its release, news broke that investigators were planning to charge Jackson with felony child molestation. CBS canceled a Michael Jackson television special, Sony cut back on promotions, and sales tanked.

Contrast this with the good fortune enjoyed in 2003 by the Bertelsman Group, which owns Jive Records, the label for Britney Spears. Already an international superstar, Spears scaled new heights when she and Madonna shared a televised wet kiss during the Grammy Awards. Her album *In the Zone* was also released on November 18, 2003, but unlike *Number Ones*, it shot straight up the charts.

There is an element of luck in every business venture. Demand can change for reasons that cannot reasonably be predicted. Costs can fluctuate due to unexpected shortages and surpluses. Firms can insulate themselves against some unexpected volatility, but this is often impractical and may not even be desirable. (Shareholders who want to diversify risk can hold a broad portfolio of stocks; managers of individual firms need not diversify the risk for them.)

Once we recognize the importance of luck, we can apply some simple statistical logic to see how it affects sustainability. Odds are good that if a firm has outperformed its rivals in the past, part of the reason is that the firm had a little luck on its side. (It would take a truly exceptional firm to outperform its rivals while enduring a stroke of bad luck.) By the same token, poor performers usually have had at least a small dose of bad luck. By its very nature, luck does not persist. This means that a firm that has bad luck in one year can expect to have average luck the next; likewise for the firm blessed by good luck. The result is what statisticians call *mean regression*. Good performers one year perform slightly less well the next year; bad performers slightly better. This has nothing to do with changes in management effort or ability, or the effort and ability of competitors. It is the inevitable combination of luck and statistics.

The failure of management to recognize the importance of luck seems always to be on display in the world of sports. A few years ago, the Chicago Bears football team surprised their long-suffering fans by going 13-3 and advancing to the playoffs. The team rewarded head coach Dick Jauron with a pay hike and contract extension. After three straight losing seasons, including one 3-13 campaign, the team canned Coach Jauron in 2003 (though they had to eat much of his salary).

The truth was that the Bears were not as good as they appeared when they won 13 games, and they were probably not as bad as they seemed when they lost 13 games. During their playoff year, the Bears won several close games on the final play, including two miraculous overtime victories. During the 3-13 year, they were hit particularly hard by the injury bug, including injuries to their top three quarterbacks. Luck, both good and bad, played a large role in the fate of Coach Jauron and the Chicago Bears.

What does this have to do with sustaining advantage? If there is a large element of luck in the success of many business ventures, then we should see substantial volatility in performance, for reasons that have nothing to do with managerial skill. This is not to say that all changes in organizational performance, for better or for worse, should be chalked up to luck. Rather, we are merely cautioning against attributing fluctuations in a firm's fortunes to improvements or deterioration of management skill.

WRAPPING UP

If achieving a competitive advantage is difficult, sustaining that advantage may be even harder. The firm must produce more B–C than its rivals, survive competition and entry, and minimize the effects of imitation. Isolating mechanisms such as reputation, switching costs, and early-mover advantages can help, but they are not panaceas. What works for some firms in some markets may be fruitless for others. Table 8.2

Table 8.2
Exploiting Isolated Mechanisms

Advantage	Markets Where This Matters	Feedback Effects	Provisos
Experience Advantage (Firm Learning Curve)	• Acquiring learning within the used production process is difficult. • Applying process learning drives costs down markedly.	Firm undercuts rival in price, thereby gaining additional volume and cumulative experience.	Human resources management strategies are critical to success of learning firms.
Product Track Record (Consumer Experience)	• This is an experience good market. • It is otherwise costly for consumers to discern quality prior to purchase.	The firm's consumer base is sticky, thereby serving to increase the firm's credibility with undecided or new consumers.	New ways for consumers to solve the shopping problem may emerge.
Switching Costs	• Consumers have invested in or accumulated assets (for example, a stock of knowledge) particular to using the firm's product. • The consumers' accumulated assets increase their B of using the firm's product.	The longer the firm has had a consumer, the more that consumer has invested and consequently the less likely that consumer is to go to another firm.	Much easier to talk about than implement.
Installed Base (Network Externalities)	• Consumers get more B the higher the number of customers the firm serves.	The larger is your installed base and the more attractive is the market to complementary good suppliers, the more consumers you then attract.	Competition for the market can destroy the value of the market.

summarizes many of the issues that firms will face when pondering the establishment of isolating mechanisms.

NOTES

1. While at NBC, Tarses oversaw the development of megahits *Friends* and *Frasier*. She was not at ABC long before the Disney acquisition and was soon engaged in power struggles. On leaving Disney/ABC, a bitter Tarses said, "I don't want to play anymore."

2. P. Milgrom and J. Roberts, "The Economics of Modern Manufacturing: Technology, Strategy, and Organization," *American Economic Review* 80(6) (1990): pp. 511–528.

3. Quoted in "He Who Moves First Finishes Last," http://www.fastcompany.com/online/38/cdu.html. (Searched 7/20/2004.)

4. The latest trend is to begin with cels and then advance to computer images. The old-fashioned animation trade is not completely lost.

5. This is described in detail by C. L. Benkard, "Learning and Forgetting: The Dynamics of Aircraft Production," New Haven: Yale University, 1998, mimeo.

6. Internet communities have established some niche auction sites. For example, audiogon.com is the favorite choice of audiophiles, and lists many more hi-end components than can be found at eBay. This web site succeeds, in part, because of the network effect enjoyed by the largest audiophile chat site, audioasylum.com, whose thousands of regular users also represent a major group of buyers and sellers and audiogon.

7. In virtually all models of oligopoly, the profits of a monopolist exceed the sum of the profits of duopolists.

CHAPTER 9

TWO EXAMPLES OF STRATEGY IN ACTION: SOUTHWEST AIRLINES AND THE CHICAGO HOSPITAL MARKET

In the first eight chapters of this book, we laid out a set of concepts for evaluating a firm's position, the competitive landscape, and long run threats to its viability. This is the core set of knowledge required to craft and evaluate strategy. In this chapter, we apply these concepts to two distinct strategy problems. The first considers the growth and current position of Southwest Airlines, an exemplar of strategic positioning in a notoriously unforgiving market. The second examines evolving opportunities for value creation in the Chicago hospital market. The Southwest example emphasizes concepts and tools used to evaluate positioning and sustainability. The hospital example focuses more on concepts for evaluating evolving competitive conditions and firms' responses to change.

SOUTHWEST AIRLINES

It is hard to find a strategy book that does not profile Southwest Airlines (herein SWA). This may be well-trodden terrain, but we have decided to include an evaluation of SWA's strategy for a few reasons. The first is that Southwest is an example of a firm that has performed well in an industry

that has otherwise performed exceptionally poorly. Even prior to Sep-
tember 11, 2001, major carriers were flying in and out of bankruptcy,
with few if any showing positive returns on investor capital. (See Figure
9.1.) That is, SWA crafted a strategy that actually *overcame* pernicious industry conditions. Hence, SWA provides an opportunity for us to drive
home the point that strategy *really* matters: If a good strategy can deliver
profits in a bad environment, a good strategy can always contribute sig-
nificantly to profits. Second, many analysts claim to identify *the reason* for
SWA's success. But the B–C framework shows us that success did not
come simply to SWA; value creation was hard work, and defending its
superior position has been even harder.

While there is little doubt that the success of SWA can be traced to
specific strategic initiatives, we believe the sources of the firm's success
are often oversimplified in both trade and academic journals. Analysts
from various disciplines tend to ascribe SWA's success to activities that
they hold close to their hearts. Experts in organizational behavior praise

Figure 9.1
Evidence of Southwest's Excellent Performance Relative to Its Peers

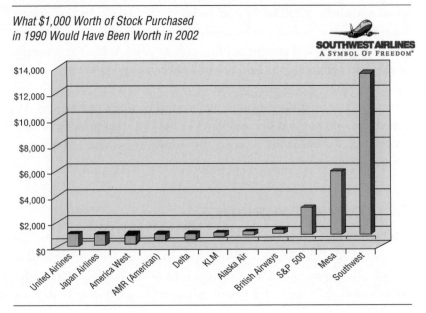

SWA's hiring practices, employee incentives, and culture of fun. Operations experts marvel at SWA's choice of a uniform fleet, the consonance of its point-to-point system with its choice of routes, and the efficiency of its turnaround procedures. Economists point to the ability of SWA to select underserved city pairs with sufficient demand to keep flights full.

While there is some truth in each of these perspectives, there must be something more to SWA's success. After all, other airlines such as Continental have successfully copied SWA's human resources practices, rivals such as Jet Blue operate a uniform fleet, and U.S. geography is hardly a trade secret. Yet somehow SWA has managed to *sustain* its superior performance, even though each of the building blocks of its success is imitable. Furthermore, this is not a story of "each component on its own is imitable but recreating the whole is not possible." There are carriers that have emulated with great success several of SWA's policies and procedures mixed in with some new ideas that have resulted in even lower costs. Yet SWA has enjoyed sustained profits for the better part of three decades. Even so, SWA is now facing the same economic crunch due to rising fuel prices that is harming the rest of the industry. Although SWA appears to be in better shape than most of its competition, its future is uncertain. For the first time, SWA's strategic dominance is no longer certain. We use our strategy frameworks to understand why SWA succeeded for so long, and explain why things may be changing.

SOME INDUSTRY JARGON

A bit of jargon will facilitate our discussion of SWA. Airline costs fall into three broad categories:

1. *Flight-sensitive costs* vary with the number of flights the airline offers. These include the costs associated with crews and servicing aircraft. Once the airline sets its schedule, these costs are fixed.
2. *Traffic-sensitive costs* vary with the number of passengers. These include the costs associated with items such as ticketing agents and food. To a lesser extent, fuel costs are also traffic-sensitive. Airlines plan their expenditures on these items in anticipation of the level of traffic, but in the short run, these costs are also fixed (with the

exception of fuel costs, which vary slightly with the number of passengers).

3. *Fixed-overhead costs* include general and administrative expenses, costs associated with marketing and advertising, and interest expenses.

The largest category of costs is flight-sensitive. When combined with fixed-overhead costs, we make the important observation that once an airline has set its schedule, nearly all of its costs are fixed and thus unavoidable. This has immediate implications for pricing. Since it is better to generate cash flow to cover some fixed costs rather than to cover none at all, an airline will be willing to fly passengers at prices far below its average total cost. The result is that the incidence of price wars during periods of low demand is likely to be greater in this industry than in most others. Indeed, airfares (and industry performance) are very pro-cyclical.

Industry analysts use two alternative measures of an airline's costs:

1. Cost per available seat-mile (ASM).
2. Cost per revenue-passenger mile (RPM).

Cost per ASM is an airline's operating costs divided by the total number of seat-miles it flies.[1] It is essentially the cost per unit of *capacity*. Cost per RPM is the airline's operating costs divided by the number of revenue-passenger miles it flies.[2] It is essentially the cost per unit of *actual output*. Airlines also talk about their *load factor*. This is the fraction of seats an airline fills on its flights. ASM, RPM, and load factor are related by the following formula:

$$\text{Cost per RPM} = \text{cost per ASM} \div \text{load factor}$$

All of these variables are important to airlines. But in the end, an airline must be able to set prices in excess of their costs per RPM if they are to turn a profit.

Airlines differ greatly in their cost per ASM and cost per RSM. For example, SWA's cost per ASM and cost per RSM are about 20 percent (or 2 to 3 cents) below the industry average. Differences across airlines in cost per ASM reflect differences in:

- Average length of flights (cost per ASM declines with distance).
- Fleet composition (cost per ASM is smaller with bigger planes).
- Input prices, especially wage rates.
- Input productivity, especially labor.
- Overall operating efficiency.

Two airlines might have very similar costs per ASM, but quite different costs per RPM because of differences in load factor. For example, ATA's current cost per ASM is about 20 percent below that for United Airlines. But ATA's current load factor of 70 percent (about 70 percent of its seats are filled) compares unfavorably with United's load factor of 85 percent. The result is that both carriers have similar costs per RSM, and both are in bankruptcy.

AIRLINE MARKET DEFINITION

Chapter 5 discusses the importance of market definition for industry analysis. Market definition can also be vital for studying firm positioning, especially for firms like SWA that serve specific target markets. Before we forge ahead with our discussion of positioning, it is worth taking time out to define airline markets. The domestic passenger airline industry is not a single monolithic market. Instead, it consists of thousands of origin–destination pairs. Passengers flying from Boston to Miami would not consider a flight from Chicago to Denver to be a viable substitute. Thus, competition occurs at the level of each city pair. This makes it possible for even a small airline to dominate its market, assuming it chooses its markets wisely.

The hub-and-spoke system pioneered by American Airlines and emulated successfully by United, Delta, and others, facilitates travel between virtually all cities with airports, by routing passengers into large hubs such as Chicago's O'Hare Airport. This adds time and inconvenience to travel, and SWA made its mark partly by providing nonstop alternatives (known as point-to-point travel) to passengers who otherwise would have to fly through hubs.

Another SWA strategy has been to operate out of the secondary airports in major metropolitan areas (such as Oakland Airport in the Bay Area and Midway Airport in Chicago). SWA competes with carriers flying out of the major airports, but the competition is softened due to customer preferences for specific airports based on location and convenience.

SOUTHWEST AIRLINES THROUGH THE B–C FRAMEWORK

We are now prepared to use the B–C framework to understand how SWA creates more value than its competitors.

Costs

The common impression is that SWA's success is due to its cost advantage. The truth is more complex and more interesting. Even so, there is something to the argument that SWA enjoys an inimitable cost advantage. In other words, SWA's efficiencies are essential to SWA's success, but its success is not due solely to its efficiencies. Thus, we begin by identifying several of the key factors that have contributed to SWA's superior cost position (in no particular order).

Low Turnaround Time Turnaround time is the time from when a plane lands to when it takes off again. SWA's low turnaround time is legendary.[3] Due to a variety of factors (use of uncongested airports, early check-in, minimal food service), SWA can turn a plane in less than 30 minutes relative to the industry average of more than 45 minutes. Turnaround time is a nontrivial driver of a carrier's costs. Consider a carrier with 2,000 flights per day that uses each of its planes for 10 hours per day. If the carrier turned planes in 30 minutes rather than 45 minutes, the carrier would save 500 hours per day turning aircraft. It would need to own 50 fewer airplanes (500 hours/10 hours per day of flying per plane) to offer the same number of RPMs. If each plane costs, say, $50 million, this would translate into a savings of $2.5 billion in assets. At any cost of capital, this is quite an advantage!

Standardized Fleet SWA's fleet of 737s enables more efficient maintenance of its aircraft. Maintenance personnel can develop a deep expertise in a single type of aircraft. Furthermore, the carrier can hold a leaner inventory of parts than would be the case if multiple models of planes needed to be serviced. Also noteworthy is that SWA's fleet is young relative to the age of many other carriers' fleets.

Labor Costs SWA pays wages that are below the industry average.[4] Even so, SWA employees are among the most satisfied in the industry, because there are many other aspects of working for SWA that its employees value highly. Thanks to its route structure, SWA pilots and flight attendants spend more evenings at home. Thanks to its low fares, popular routes, and loyal customers, SWA's business is somewhat less cyclical than the industry norm, leading to fewer employee layoffs during downturns. With few long haul flights, SWA can offer more flexible working hours. SWA aggressively promotes from within, opening a career path to its low wage workers. SWA also has a reputation for a "LUVing" work environment.[5] Finally, SWA operates in some markets where employees have few attractive outside options. In other words, even if other carriers matched SWA's human resources practices for flexibility, time at home, and so on, they would still be at a disadvantage due to SWA's location.

Cross-Utilized Labor Force Early on, SWA negotiated with its unions (yes, SWA is unionized) to allow multitasking. Thus, the worker who guides planes to and from gates may also unload baggage. The flight attendant may also handle gate announcements and check-in. This results in substantially less employee downtime, especially at relatively uncongested airports where there may not be enough flights to keep a specialized worker busy all the time.

This represents only a partial list of the factors that hold down costs at SWA. SWA also saves money by avoiding travel agent commissions, eliminating hub-and-spoke service (thereby cutting down on baggage handling), and using secondary airports with minimal slotting and gate fees.

Benefits

To some extent, it seems that SWA's cost reductions have come at the *expense* of customer benefits. SWA does not assign seats. It does not serve food. It does not allow bookings through travel agents. It has minimal baggage handling capabilities. Yet the effect on B is minimal, largely because much of what SWA eliminates is unlikely to be missed very much on an SWA flight. The typical SWA passenger, flying perhaps 75 minutes between Dallas and New Orleans, does not feel too stung by a bad seat, is not very much interested in a meal, does not need a travel agent, and probably does not have much luggage. In other words, SWA has avoided *overserving* its customers. Given its route structure, this is entirely appropriate.

SWA does have some features that are associated with higher B (at least for some customer segments). Two are frequent departures and funny, sassy employees.

Frequent Departures At one time, more than 85 percent of SWA growth came from increasing the density of flights *within* existing routes as opposed to the introduction of new routes. Hence on the routes SWA serves, fliers tend to have a large number of departures to choose from. This is especially valuable to high paying business travelers who require the flexibility to adjust their schedules at a moment's notice. We know of anecdotes of firms that have sought out customers and/or suppliers based on SWA's route structure.

Funny, Sassy Employees We are a little uncomfortable with this one, as there are flyers who truly despise levity. But for those who appreciate it, the feature comes at a very low cost.

We are not suggesting that SWA has both lower C and higher B. Rather, we believe that SWA offers substantially lower C and, for its route structure, only fractionally lower B. The result is a higher B–C, and that is what matters most for strategic positioning.

Summary: A Resources and Capabilities Audit

We can summarize our discussion of B–C by completing an R&C audit (Table 9.1). Note that scopability in this case refers to the ability to expand into new geographic markets.

Table 9.1
Resources and Capabilities Audit for Southwest Airlines

Resource/ Capability	Is It Scarce?	Is It Mobile?	Is It Scopable?	Is It a Source of Enduring Advantage?
Route Structure	Yes	No	Partial[a]	Yes
Uniform Fleet	No	No[b]	Yes[c]	No
Labor Force	Somewhat[d]	No	Yes	Somewhat

[a]Southwest can add point-to-point flights from current cities it serves, but has limited ability to route through hubs.
[b]Boeing cannot raise the price of 737s, despite Southwest's reliance on that plane, because Boeing also sells the plane to many other carriers, and must be competitive with the Airbus 319 and 320.
[c]Latest generation 737s capable of transcontinental flight.
[d]Union rules at Southwest are much more flexible than at established carriers, but changes at competitors brought about by bankruptcy are closing the gap.

We conclude that Southwest's route structure is critical to its success. (In fact, it is Southwest's route structure that allows it to operate a uniform fleet.) Hub-and-spoke carriers require larger planes for popular long haul flights (e.g., New York to Los Angeles) but must operate small planes for flights to hub cities (e.g., Los Angeles to Sacramento). This posited success is backed up by the facts: SWA has lower costs and higher operating margins than any other major competitor. (In many years, SWA is the only major carrier to turn a profit!)

SUSTAINABILITY

Now we have a bit of a puzzle. Compared with other carriers, SWA offers lower C and comparable B. It enjoys higher profits as a result. Why, then, don't other carriers mimic its operations and success? For carriers like United, Delta, and American, the answer is simple. They set up hub-and-spoke networks decades ago, and these networks do not allow them to match SWA's business practices. The hub-and-spoke system is much maligned for associated delays and lost baggage. It also requires flying out of large cities that have high labor costs. This makes it seem that hub-and-spoke operations are woefully inefficient, and in terms of cost per ASM, they may be. But what matters most is cost per RPM, and here is where hub-and-spoke can really shine.

Recall that cost per ASM depends on cost per RSM and the load factor. Southwest's many cost advantages contribute to a lower cost per RSM. But the hub-and-spoke system was designed to boost the load factor. Consider flying from, say, Albany to Sacramento. There is not nearly enough demand to fill a transcontinental airplane flying this route nonstop. But United Airlines can fly smaller planes from feeder cities like Albany into and out of hub cities like Chicago. By adding other passengers flying out of Albany to destinations worldwide (and passengers flying from all over the world into Sacramento), United can fill its planes on both legs of the Albany to Sacramento trip.

As long as point-to-point carriers such as SWA do not cherry pick too many nonstop routes, the hub-and-spoke giants can maintain higher load factors and be cost competitive. Unfortunately for United et al., steady population growth, combined with new smaller airplanes capable of long haul trips (including new long haul 737s), have increased the number of profitable point-to-point routes. The erosion of feeder traffic from spokes to hubs has fundamentally changed industry economics. United et al. are slowly ceding medium-sized markets to SWA and its imitators; they now see their future in dominating traffic in hub cities and especially in international flights, where their U.S. routes serve as feeders to international hubs such as Washington–Dulles and New York–JFK.

We can understand why the hub-and-spoke carriers were reluctant to mimic SWA. But why hasn't SWA been assaulted by more upstarts like Jet Blue and even United's Ted than we have observed up to this point? The answer lies, to a large extent, in specific tactics adopted by SWA to defend its position. Consider again SWA's route selection and its choice to saturate those routes with frequent departures. When entering underserved markets, Southwest could have charged high monopoly prices. But it instead exploited its low costs by setting low prices. Because many of the markets had price sensitive customers (many SWA passengers consider driving to be a reasonable alternative), this expanded the market tremendously (there was a fivefold increase in RPMs out of some SWA cities).

By themselves, the increased volumes may or may not have been the profit maximizing option (as opposed to SWA selecting higher prices and realizing lower volumes). But frequent flights have enabled SWA to maintain a dominant position at its secondary airports. Passengers get more B when there are more departure choices, and by becoming the first high-volume, low price carrier in the smaller airports it served, SWA prevents a second firm from employing a similar strategy. In particular, it has been very important that SWA establish dominance in airports that are not large enough to support a similar-sized rival. This gives SWA a substantial first-mover advantage. Over the years, carriers such as Midway Airlines, Midwest Express, America West, and Jet Blue have attempted to copy some or all of SWA's tactics, but they rarely attempt to enter SWA's markets. Ironically, SWA stands to inherit dozens of gates at Chicago's Midway Airport abandoned by upstart ATA, whose aggressive growth strategy coincided with the post-9/11 industry downturn and forced the carrier into bankruptcy.

Today, SWA's star is shining a little less brightly. It has suffered from the same oil price shock that affected the rest of the industry. Some of the markets it once dominated have grown to where competitors have established footholds. It entered into some markets, such as California, where established hub-and-spoke carriers have put up considerable resistance. But some of its problems reflect the limitations of its chosen tactics:

- The promise of promotion may have helped SWA hire workers at lower pay, but it requires nonstop growth lest promotion opportunities dry up. There are only so many underserved city pairs, and entry by newcomers (and spinoffs such as Ted) further limits growth opportunities.
- The hub-and-spoke carriers have exploited their financial troubles to extract wage concessions from unions, reducing the cost gap.
- While it made sense for SWA to select a single type of airplane, this tactic requires the continued use of outmoded Boeing 737s, and SWA's aging fleet is no longer as fuel efficient.

A decade ago, Herb Kelleher questioned whether SWA could continue to grow while maintaining its strategic position. It is not SWA's fault that its future is a little less bright; even the best strategies have limitations that are ultimately exposed. But the strategies and tactics used by SWA to create and defend its superior position earned a rightful place in the lore of business strategy. SWA's success was due not simply to culture or operations or monopoly power, but rather to a combination of these and other factors, tied together by the insight that a strategy of entering underserved markets, implemented in just the right way, could provide enduring value.

ER: RESTORING HEALTH TO THE CHICAGO HOSPITAL MARKET

It has been a turbulent two decades for America's community hospitals.[6] Through the mid-1980s, almost all of the nation's 6,000 community hospitals showed positive operating margins and rapid growth. Since then, a variety of factors combined to take their toll on hospital finances. About 75 hospitals a year have gone bankrupt, leaving fewer than 5,000 community hospitals today. In the past few years, however, hospital profit margins are on the rise, and new hospitals are springing up, especially in wealthy suburban markets.

Hospitals in the Chicago area have been battered by the same forces that affected hospitals nationwide. More than a dozen of the area's hospitals have closed in the past two decades and others have merged in the hope of avoiding the same fate. But the financial outlook has brightened. At least five existing hospitals have plans to build new facilities in rapidly growing suburban communities, and some downtown hospitals are rapidly expanding as well. By examining the changing face of hospital competition, we can better understand why Chicago-area hospitals have been on such a roller coaster ride. At the same time, we can identify and evaluate various strategies and tactics for surviving and thriving as the market continues to evolve.

COMPETITOR IDENTIFICATION

Industry analysis begins with competitor identification. This requires careful consideration of both product and geographic markets. Community hospitals are multiproduct firms, providing a range of therapeutic and surgical services as well as diagnostic and routine medical services. Some hospitals also offer maternity care, neonatology, psychiatric care, and pediatrics. Others focus on cardiac care or cancer. Although competition in each product segment is played out slightly differently, we avoid these distinctions in favor of emphasizing common themes across the segments.

Over the past 20 years, hospitals have faced growing competition in some product segments from physicians and other entrepreneurs who offer minor surgery and diagnostic services in private offices or other outpatient facilities. While any hospital manager should be concerned about losing business to outpatient providers, the bread and butter services for community hospitals remain those that must be provided in a hospital, where access to intensive care and state-of-the-art technologies gives hospitals the edge over outpatient providers. For the foreseeable future, community hospitals will continue to dominate the markets for cardiac surgery, joint replacements, deliveries, neurosurgery, and other big ticket items.

Geographic market definition is equally subtle. Most patients in Chicago prefer to be hospitalized close to home. Chicago highways can get very congested, which can be a severe deterrent to traveling for care. This means that Chicago hospitals compete for patients with other hospitals within a fairly short crow flies distance of, say, 10 miles. Complicating this analysis is the fact that most patients have insurance through a managed care organization (MCO) and must select a hospital that contracts with the MCO. When assembling a Chicago-area hospital network, an MCO usually includes hospitals from all parts of the metropolitan area. Failure to assemble a broad network may disqualify an MCO from consideration by firms looking to provide an attractive health benefit option to employees. This can give inordinate power to a hospital that is in a prime location and has no nearby competitors. On the other hand, patients may be willing to travel quite far to receive certain high-end treatments for which the skill of the hospital's medical staff is a critical concern. For example, transplant patients will travel from distant exurbs like Kankakee, Illinois, and Kenosha, Wisconsin, to receive treatment from one of the university hospitals in downtown Chicago.

We reach the following conclusions about competitor identification in Chicagoland:

- Chicago hospitals compete in many different product markets.
- Competition for products that are easily provided by physicians and other outpatient providers is likely to be very intense. However, there are many products, such as cardiac surgery, that remain the domain of the community hospital.
- Competition with other hospitals is likely to be local. The geographic scope of competition depends on how MCOs assemble their networks. Geographic scope may also vary by service; markets for complex treatments may have a large geographic scope.

Market Structure

We can now make some preliminary statements about market structure. (More quantitative analysis requires further analytic tools.) There are about 60 community hospitals in the Chicago area. This seems like more than enough to assure vigorous competition, but the nature of competition is limited for several reasons. First, there are many hospital systems; Advocate, the largest system, owns 10 hospitals and controls about 15 percent of the entire market. Even so, there remain dozens of distinct competitors in the metro area and the area Herfindahl is below .10. Second, competition varies by geographic region within Chicago. Community hospitals in the cental city face many competitors. Hospitals in some suburbs face relatively little competition because they either are geographically isolated or have a location that is extremely valuable to MCOs. Some seemingly small systems such as the three hospital Evanston–Northwestern Healthcare (ENH) system dominate prime geographic locations (such as the wealthy North Shore suburbs) and may possess substantial market power.

Finally, competition narrows considerably if we focus on specific services for which only a handful of hospitals have sufficient expertise. These would include high-end services such as open heart surgery and neonatology. For very specialized services such as transplantation, however, the market may extend beyond Chicagoland.

Competitive Levers

Hospitals have many levers to press when competing for patients. No one goes to a hospital for the accommodations (the Four Seasons Hotel has nicer rooms, better food, and a lower price). So we might expect hospitals to compete on the basis of their technical quality. But amenities count for something as well. Hospitals might even try to attract patients by lowering prices.

At first blush, it appears that the Chicago hospital market has many of the symptoms that would indicate the potential for destructive price competition. There are many competitors, especially within the central city. Production costs vary across hospitals, so that some hospitals may use their advantage to try to undercut their rivals. There is a history of substantial excess capacity; occupancy rates at many hospitals have averaged below 70 percent for decades.[7] Finally, demand for admissions has only recently reversed a decades-long slump. But at various times, institutional features have served to soften price competition, forcing hospitals to compete on nonprice dimensions.

Competition prior to 1990

Competition among hospitals was relatively benign until about 15 years ago. This was partly because patients had idiosyncratic preferences for hospitals based on factors such as location and religious affiliation. But the main reason had to do with health insurance. Most patients had indemnity insurance that paid almost the entire hospital bill, making price a secondary consideration. Insurance tilted the calculus of B–C creation in favor of maximizing B, almost regardless of C.

This led to competition on the basis of perceived benefits. Although patients may have cared about the ability of hospitals to treat what ailed them, hospitals competed mainly by offering a wide array of amenities, from new porticoes to valet parking and steak dinners for maternity patients. This is probably because patients had no way of knowing which hospitals had the best technical quality, and so focused on things they could observe. Hospitals understood this and invested in those dimensions of quality that would draw the biggest response.

Hospitals also realized that most patients played a secondary role in selecting where to get treatment. If hospitals wanted patients, they would need to attract patients' physicians. Hospitals reasoned that if they could enhance the productivity and earning power of physicians, the patients would follow. Thus hospitals began loading up on the latest in treatment technology and well-trained support staff. The result became known as the medical arms race (MAR) and contributed to escalating health care costs in large cities like Chicago.

From the point of view of enrollees and taxpayers (who foot the bill for Medicare and Medicaid), the MAR was a costly excess. But from the point of view of hospitals, the medical arms race was a benign way to compete, much preferred to price competition. The MAR drove costs skyward, but hospitals raised prices more than enough to compensate. Patients continued to come despite the price hikes; they had no alternative. This drove up demand for outpatient services, but many hospitals compensated by building their own outpatient facilities. For many other services, patients had little choice but to continue to visit their community hospitals. Price simply was not an issue.

Entry Barriers

In a normal market, the ongoing success of virtually all established firms would invite entry. Not so for Chicago hospitals, because entry into the market has been limited by regulation. Since the early 1970s, new hospitals must receive approval from a state health planning board. At the time the planning rules were established, reimbursement practices assured that the costs of any excess capacity would be borne by consumers and taxpayers. (Such practices helped to fuel the MAR.) The planning rules were thought necessary to stem the MAR and other unnecessary duplication of service. Although reimbursement practices have subsequently changed as we describe later, the planning rules have not, and there have been no new hospitals built in the Chicago area for several decades.[8]

COMPETITION IN THE 1990S

By 1990, MCOs had secured a strong foothold in the Chicago market, replacing the traditional indemnity insurance that had fueled the MAR.

Through a strategy known as "selective contracting," MCOs injected price competition into the market. Here is how it worked. MCOs contracted with those hospitals that offered the most favorable rates. They provided enrollees with nearly complete coverage of medical costs if they visited a "preferred provider," but required enrollees to make substantial payments if they selected "out of network" hospitals. For the first time, hospitals discovered that price would move market share. This restored the balance to B and C; given the difficulty of measuring technical quality, some might argue that it tilted the equation too far in favor of reducing C at the expense of B.

Four additional factors added to competitive pressures:

1. When forming networks, MCOs often ignored patient loyalties and treated most hospitals as undifferentiated, interchangeable parts of the network.
2. MCOs negotiated hospital prices in secret, encouraging hospitals to lower prices to win contracts.
3. Contract negotiations were infrequent (i.e., a contract lasts one to three years) and lumpy (i.e., one insurer may represent 5 percent or more of a hospital's business), further intensifying the pressure on hospitals to bid low enough to secure a place in the network.
4. Most Chicago hospitals had excess capacity and were eager to fill their beds so as to generate some contribution toward fixed costs.

Not surprisingly, price rivalry intensified and hospitals offered substantial discounts to MCOs. Competition among MCOs drove down premiums, and MCOs stole market share from traditional indemnity insurers. This further intensified the pressure on hospitals.

HOSPITAL RESPONSES TO COMPETITIVE PRESSURES

In the space of a decade, managed care enrollments in Chicago increased from 25 percent to more than 90 percent of the private insurance market. Hospitals could not abide by the status quo, where amenities and the MAR dictated a hospital's level of success, and failure was nonexistent. Hospitals had to find new ways to survive and thrive.

Cost Cutting

Prior to managed care, all the strategic emphasis was on maximizing B. Hospital executives believed that managed care would cause a 180-degree turnaround, with a near total emphasis on C.[9] Most hospitals followed the same path toward cost containment. They pursued Total Quality Management (TQM) programs. They trimmed their workforce and adapted treatment guidelines to improve the efficiency of care delivery. Hospital costs fell, but this did little to alleviate the competitive pressures from MCOs, which played hospitals off against one another in negotiations to force them to pass along their cost savings through price reductions. Consumers benefited, as hospital prices and health insurance premiums remained virtually flat during the mid-1990s. But cost cutting did little to improve the lot of hospitals. Cost reduction may have been a necessary step to remaining competitive, but it was not sufficient.

Efforts to Improve Quality

Although the MAR was nominally about competing on B, the dimensions of benefit competition were often superficial. Porticoes and steak dinners were nice, and new technologies helped, but these were easily observable product characteristics that often had little bearing on the ultimate outcome of care. No patient chooses to have surgery to get the steak dinner; what ultimately matters is whether the surgery succeeds and the patient lives. With selective contracting changing the nature of competition, hospitals began to hope that if they could deliver superior quality, superior prices would follow.

At first, quality improvement efforts were a combination of a little TQM and a lot of window dressing. A disturbing trend was when many hospitals made a few cosmetic changes to existing programs and marketed them as Centers of Excellence. There were Centers of Excellence in heart care, cancer, maternity care, and even male reproductive health. Industry observers believed that any relationship between the marketing buzz and actual excellence was mere happenstance, and hospitals lacked the hard data necessary to prove that Centers of Excellence delivered superior care. Fortunately, MCOs and patients alike were unmoved by these promotions and few Centers of Excellence yielded increases in market share. Unfortunately, the market continued to pay lip service to genuine quality competition. This would have to wait until better data were available.

Having done all they could to improve the performance of their own institutions, hospitals looked externally to gain a strategic advantage. The tactics they pursued included horizontal mergers, partnerships with physicians, and risk contracting. Taken together, these tactics were seen as the cornerstones of a new form of health care organization—the integrated delivery system (IDS). Forming an IDS was the dominant provider strategy of the 1990s. But many of the elements of this strategy failed to pan out and by the end of the decade, enthusiasm for the IDS strategy had waned.

Horizontal Mergers

Prior to the 1990s, most big city hospitals, including those in Chicago, had few if any partners. But the 1990s saw a merger wave that changed the competitive landscape. The most noticeable merger in Chicago occurred in 1995, when two faith-based hospital systems merged to form Advocate Healthcare. Advocate appears to have sufficient clout with insurers to command premium prices. There have been a few other high profile combinations. The only two hospitals in Waukegan (a far north suburb of Chicago) merged and secured substantial price increases. The merger of Evanston Hospital and Highland Park Hospital attracted considerable attention. As the two major hospitals serving Chicago's posh North Shore suburbs, no MCO could afford to drop both of them from their networks. The resulting bargaining leverage has enabled the hospitals to obtain hefty price increases, and reminds us that when it comes to health care, competition is local. In recognition of this local market power, the Federal Trade Commission is currently reviewing the Evanston/Highland Park merger to determine if it is anticompetitive.

While these and other mergers have given some Chicago hospitals considerable leverage, residents of most communities have several

nearby hospitals to choose from, and the market remains fairly competitive, at least when compared with some other big cities. Milwaukee is
dominated by three systems, Cleveland by two, and Boston by one.

Physician Partnerships

Facing MCOs that could steer patients to lower price competitors, hospitals felt it critical to further strengthen their ties to physicians. Some
hospitals purchased outright the practices of primary care physicians,
hoping to secure their referrals. Others entered strategic alliances with
their medical staffs, with the same ambitions. Some of these deals
worked, but the acquisition strategy proved to be particularly problematic, and hospitals have recently backed away from this strategy.

Physicians create value by guiding patients through the medical care
process. A simple rule of strategy is that it is difficult to succeed by acquiring the value created by others. Hospitals are not exempt from this
rule. Chicago hospitals hoped that by acquiring physicians, they would
acquire their patients. But Chicago hospitals competed against one another to buy practices, and in the process they bid up the purchase
price. By the mid-1990s, the going price for a single physician practice
was several hundred thousand dollars. Hospitals would also have to pay
ongoing costs for the physician's salary and office expenses.

To make matters worse, hospitals seemingly ignored the fact that acquiring practices was a negative sum game. The total number of hospital
patients was fixed. Moreover, this fixed pie of patients was divided after
the acquisition binge in roughly the same way as before. The only difference was that hospitals were paying for the referrals that used to be
free. Patients were not well-served either, as the market was now Balka-
nized in ways that did not necessarily promise that patients would go to
the hospital that best met their needs.

The final nail in the physician acquisition strategy coffin was the resulting value destruction that often occurs after vertical integration.
Physicians who used to be entrepreneurs found themselves working as
salaried employees of large companies. Productivity of acquired practices fell by as much as 10 percent, and many hospitals found themselves
losing money on nearly every acquired practice.

There were some benefits from physician acquisition, in the form of joint ventures in developing new services and simplified contracting with MCOs, but these were not sufficient to offset the aforementioned losses. Even so, hospitals were reluctant to sell off their practices. In a true prisoner's dilemma, hospitals would rather pay for referrals than allow a competitor to do the same. As it turns out, hospitals that acquired and held on to physician practices may finally be poised to realize a big payoff. But we defer this part of our analysis until after examining some of the other strategic responses to market pressures.

Risk Contracting

Traditionally, health insurers have borne the risk of high medical expenditures. They collect premiums up front, pay medical expenses as they occur, and can suffer heavy losses if the latter exceed the former. During the mid-1990s, price competition among MCOs drove down premiums to the point where the typical plan suffered operating losses of −3 percent. Yet during this period, some hospital managers were convinced that insurers were reaping undeserved profits for taking on the simple task of risk bearing. These managers believed that they could make vast fortunes by cutting out the middleman and bearing the risk themselves. What they learned instead was a bitter lesson in the basics of business strategy.

Risk bearing is not a trivial undertaking. Insurers spend considerable effort and expense performing *medical underwriting*: trying to predict future expenditures based on demographics and past trends. This is a complex task requiring enormous amounts of historical data on enrollee utilization patterns. Large insurers have these data and the experience to work with them; hospitals do not. Not surprisingly, many hospitals proved to be inept at this critical task. The result was a kind of winner's curse: Hospitals overoptimistically believed that they could keep costs below premiums. Insurers were more than willing to cater to this view, and hospitals ended up with pools of patients who were sicker and more costly to treat than hospitals had anticipated.

Insurers also have expertise in sales. To their credit, most risk contracting hospitals recognized that they lacked this capability and left sales to the insurers. In a typical arrangement, the insurer collected premiums from an employer and paid roughly 80 percent to the risk-contracting hospital. That hospital was responsible for all medical costs, while the insurer used the remaining 20 percent to cover sales expenses and profits. (The insurer was not really insuring anything anymore, merely collecting a fee for administrative services.) The result was entirely predictable. Insurers no longer cared about medical costs, and curtailed their medical underwriting. Hospitals ended up with sicker patients than they had bargained for. Hospitals found themselves suffering extraordinary losses on risk-contracting products—often exceeding −10 percent.

TODAY'S COMPETITIVE LANDSCAPE

Despite many missteps, the future for Chicago hospitals is bright. This has a lot to do with changes that the hospitals themselves have had little to do with. But a few hospitals are beginning to realize the fruits of the IDS strategy, a decade late, but welcome nonetheless.

The Managed Care Backlash

Many of hospitals' competitive woes can be traced to the growth of managed care and selective contracting. In the past few years, in an apparent backlash against managed care, employees have demanded broader networks and access to their hometown hospital. This has strengthened the hands of hospitals negotiating contracts with MCOs. At the same time, demand for hospitals has increased substantially, especially in Chicago's suburbs where growing population and aging baby boomers are keeping many hospitals filled near capacity. Proposals to build new hospitals in the fastest growing communities have been blunted by planning laws, with existing hospitals doing a heavy dose of lobbying on behalf of the status quo. To top it off, a number of local competitors have merged. The combination of growing demand, consolidation, and entry barriers has added to the pricing pressure. The result is three consecutive years of double-digit price increases and swelling hospital profit margins.

Favorable competitive forces have taken the pressure off hospitals for the time being. But the pendulum may swing back toward more intense price competition, for several reasons.

1. First and foremost, skyrocketing insurance premiums may cause employers and employees to once again consider tighter networks and access restrictions.
2. The Federal Trade Commission may win in its effort to break up the Evanston/Northwestern network, and could target other area partnerships.
3. Both the federal Medicare and Illinois Medicaid programs may sharply cut back on hospital payments to cut into looming deficits.
4. A recent corruption scandal involving the state health planning board threatens to limit their power to block new hospital construction.

Should these events transpire, Chicago hospitals will once again have to find ways to create value and soften competition. Fortunately, they are increasingly positioned to do so, largely because some of the old IDS initiatives are beginning to bear fruit.

Information Technology, Value Creation, and Competition

Many hospitals made big gambles during the 1990s to build integrated delivery systems. It was not unusual for a hospital to invest $10 million or more in physician practice acquisition and information technology. They have seen little return on these investments thus far, but things are changing. Hospitals that have stuck it out may soon find themselves positioned to deliver on the promise of the IDS. At the same time, an unexpectedly high degree of fragmentation among information systems may have the unintended consequence of permanently softening competition.

In their rush to acquire physicians in the 1990s, most hospitals ignored the golden rule of positioning. They paid handsomely for the value they acquired, but did not create additional value. This was not entirely their fault. Some far thinking hospital managers viewed physician integration as part of a broader strategy to overhaul the medical care process from the first time the seriously ill patient visited a primary care physician until the time when the patient left the intensive care unit and was ready to return home. Hospitals believed that physician integration was essential for coordination of the many steps in between.

The concept of coordination was sound. There is a tremendous amount of waste in the medical care system, much of it due to providers lacking the right information and the right resources when they need them. Coordination could eliminate this waste, and simultaneously boost quality. But the execution was flawed, because hospitals were missing an essential ingredient to pull it off. Coordination would require information giving physicians access to a patient's complete and up-to-the-minute medical history, and the ability to communicate instantly with other providers. Hospitals would also require information about clinical decision making and outcomes to establish best practices and instill the proper incentives for physicians to follow them. Finally, the clinical information would need to be linked to billing information to assure that the necessary services would be covered by insurance.

All of this would require integrated clinical and financial records. Although industry leaders had been talking for decades about integrating electronic clinical and financial records across a range of providers, the technology had not yet caught up with the talk. For all the efforts to integrate, care remains fragmented across providers, and real-time communication with MCOs is virtually nonexistent.

Information technology has finally turned the corner, however, and coordination of care within provider organizations and between providers and insurers is becoming a reality. But there is a hitch. The market is offering competing information technologies, and they are not compatible. Thus, providers in the Evanston–Northwestern Healthcare system can instantly transmit vital clinical and financial data to one another, and providers in Advocate can do the same, but the two systems cannot talk to each other. Thus far, neither government efforts nor market-based network effects have fixed this glaring problem.

For the time being, this fragmentation gives a leg up to hospitals that have acquired physician practices. By integrating physicians into their organizations, systems like Evanston–Northwestern and Advocate can more easily put in place a unified information system. Integration assures compatibility with member physicians and thus promotes coordination. In this way, integrated systems will finally be able to create value, rather than just transfer value from one player to another.

Fragmentation will also have a long-term strategic benefit for hospitals. Patients who wish to switch providers will find that their medical records will not easily switch with them. The resulting switching costs will make it impossible for payers to pretend that there are no points of differentiation among providers. Broad networks, and the resulting power bestowed upon providers, will be the norm.

Other looming changes may alter the competitive landscape. Employers are applying new analytic tools to large medical claims databases to perform sophisticated quality evaluations. The resulting rankings help employees select the best hospitals, but also serve as a point of differentiation for the best hospitals. Historically, only teaching hospitals could expect to receive a quality premium, and that was based solely on reputation. In the future, all hospitals will have a chance to prove their quality and reap the rewards. Given the well-documented experience curve in medical quality, we should expect many Chicago hospitals to pursue niche specialties—creating genuine Centers of Excellence.

THE FUTURE

The information revolution in health care is likely to rationalize both value creation and demand. The days when price was irrelevant and the quality of the housekeeping staff was more important than the quality of the medical staff are long gone. So, too, are strategies developed more out of desperation than inspiration, based more on buying value than on value creation. Hospital managers have learned some hard lessons but seem poised to seize the future.

Technical quality finally has its rewards. Employers are actually demanding outcomes data and paying premium prices to hospitals that can prove their worth. At the same time, employees have hammered home the importance of local access, allowing even average quality community hospitals to hold their own in contract negotiations, provided they face little competition. This may not be of much help to Chicago hospitals in the central city, which will still have a hard time distinguishing themselves from the crowd, and are especially susceptible to Medicaid cutbacks. But teaching hospitals, hospitals in systems that have invested wisely in information technology, and hospitals in wealthy suburbs are all poised for many years of success.

A few roadblocks do lie ahead. If state planning rules unravel, there could be a renewal of price competition in suburban markets, as new hospitals undo the local monopolies enjoyed by incumbents. Finally, further price increases might cause consumers to reevaluate the B–C equation. If consumers devalue health care access or quality, then all bets are off, and a return to the intense price competition of the 1990s is possible.

NOTES

1. One seat flown one mile counts as a seat-mile, whether or not it is occupied.

2. A revenue-passenger mile is one passenger flown one mile.

3. For many years, SWA was the industry leader in turnaround time. Others have learned from SWA, however, but it still ranks near the top.

4. This claim is frequently made and can be substantiated, but comparisons across carriers typically exclude the value of employee stock ownership.

5. The FAA code for SWA's home Love Field is LUV.

6. Community hospitals are open to all patients and treat a wide range of conditions. Most hospitals are community hospitals. Exceptions would include Veteran's Administration hospitals and psychiatric specialty hospitals.

7. Considering that most hospitals experience declines in census over weekends, a hospital is considered "full" if its average occupancy rate exceeds 80 percent to 85 percent.

8. During 2004, the state planning board approved two new hospital projects in the northwest and southwest suburbs.

9. Actually, cost containment began a few years prior to the growth of managed care, following changes in Medicare hospital payment rules in 1983. The growth of managed care magnified the need for cost cutting.

INDEX